TABS Assessment Tool

Temperament and Atypical Behavior Scale

Early Childhood Indicators of Developmental Dysfunction

Stephen J. Bagnato, Ed.D., N.C.S.P.
John T. Neisworth, Ph.D.
John Salvia, D.Ed.
Frances M. Hunt, Ph.D.

Instructions for administering the TABS Assessment Tool:

Please refer to Chapter 3 of the **TABS Manual** for important information before administering the TABS Assessment Tool. Complete (or have rater complete) the information in Section I. Read and discuss directions for Section II with the rater, making sure that he or she understands how to respond to the items. Ask the rater to return the Assessment Tool for scoring and interpretation when he or she has completed Section II.

I. CHILD INFORMATION

Name of child: ______________________ Sex: Female ❑ Male ❑

Date of birth: ______________________ Age (in years and months): ______________________

Child's address: ______________________

Name of parent or primary caregiver in household: ______________________

Relationship to child: Mother ❑ Father ❑ Other ______________________

Telephone number: ______________________ Best time to contact: ______________________

List any previously identified problems or diagnoses for this child.

1. ______________________
2. ______________________
3. ______________________

II. TABS INDICATORS

The following 55 items list some of the most frequent problems in temperament and self-regulation that parents and professionals observe in young children. Read each numbered item and check *No* if the behavior is not a problem. Check *Yes* if the behavior is a problem. For those items marked *Yes*, check *Need Help* if there is special concern and assistance is needed to cope with the behavior. Return this form to the individual administering this Assessment Tool for scoring and interpretation.

Name of rater: ______________________ Date Assessment Tool completed: ______________________

Relationship to child: ______________________

DETACHED

DETACHED	No	Yes	Need Help
1. Consistently upset by changes in schedule	☐	☐	☐
2. Emotions don't match what is going on	☐	☐	☐
3. Seems to look through or past people	☐	☐	☐
4. Resists looking you in the eye	☐	☐	☐
5. Acts like others are not there	☐	☐	☐
6. Hardly ever starts on own to play with others	☐	☐	☐
7. Moods and wants are too hard to figure out	☐	☐	☐
8. Seems to be in "own world"	☐	☐	☐
9. Often stares into space	☐	☐	☐
10. "Tunes out," loses contact with what is going on	☐	☐	☐
11. Plays with toys in strange ways	☐	☐	☐
12. Plays with toys as if confused by how they work	☐	☐	☐
13. Makes strange throat noises	☐	☐	☐
14. Disturbed by too much light, noise, or touching	☐	☐	☐
15. Overexcited in crowded places	☐	☐	☐
16. Stares at lights	☐	☐	☐
17. Overly interested in toy/object	☐	☐	☐
18. Flaps hands over and over	☐	☐	☐
19. Shakes head over and over	☐	☐	☐
20. Wanders around without purpose	☐	☐	☐

Detached Raw Score → ☐

HYPER-SENSITIVE/ACTIVE

HYPER-SENSITIVE/ACTIVE	No	Yes	Need Help
21. Upset by every little thing	☐	☐	☐
22. Often difficult to soothe when upset and crying	☐	☐	☐
23. Has wide swings in mood	☐	☐	☐
24. Gets angry too easily	☐	☐	☐
25. Too easily frustrated	☐	☐	☐
26. Has wild temper tantrums	☐	☐	☐
27. Frequently irritable, "touchy," or fussy	☐	☐	☐
28. Can't wait at all for food or toy	☐	☐	☐
29. Demands attention continually	☐	☐	☐
30. Controls adult's behavior, "is the boss"	☐	☐	☐

	No	Yes	Need Help
31. Jealous too often	☐	☐	☐
32. Mostly on the go, "in high gear"	☐	☐	☐
33. Doesn't sit still	☐	☐	☐
34. Too "grabby," impulsive	☐	☐	☐
35. Almost always refuses to do what is told	☐	☐	☐
36. Throws or breaks things on purpose	☐	☐	☐
37. Bites, hits, kicks others	☐	☐	☐

Hyper-sensitive/active Raw Score → ☐

UNDERREACTIVE

	No	Yes	Need Help
38. Rarely smiles, giggles, or laughs at funny things	☐	☐	☐
39. Doesn't pay attention to sights and sounds	☐	☐	☐
40. Doesn't seem to watch moving objects	☐	☐	☐
41. Shows no surprise to new events	☐	☐	☐
42. Doesn't react to own name	☐	☐	☐
43. Doesn't care when others are hurt	☐	☐	☐
44. Doesn't play much at all	☐	☐	☐
45. Doesn't enjoy playing with mother or caregiver	☐	☐	☐
46. Isn't upset when toy is taken away	☐	☐	☐
47. Almost never babbles or tries to talk	☐	☐	☐
48. Doesn't react to sounds	☐	☐	☐

Underreactive Raw Score → ☐

DYSREGULATED

	No	Yes	Need Help
49. Often cries too long	☐	☐	☐
50. Often frightened by dreams or the nighttime	☐	☐	☐
51. Screams in sleep and can't be comforted	☐	☐	☐
52. Can't comfort self when upset	☐	☐	☐
53. Wakes up often and doesn't fall back asleep	☐	☐	☐
54. Doesn't have a regular sleep schedule	☐	☐	☐
55. Too often needs help to fall asleep	☐	☐	☐

Dysregulated Raw Score → ☐

III. RESULTS

Add the items marked *Yes* in each of the four subtests, and place the totals in the appropriate boxes marked Raw Score (e.g., *Detached Raw Score*) after each subtest. Transfer those totals to the spaces under the column titled Raw Scores below. Add the four raw scores to calculate the *Temperament & Regulatory Index (TRI),* and place it in the space provided. Determine percentiles and standard scores (or T-scores) of each of these raw scores by using the Conversion Table in the appendix in the **TABS Manual**. (Refer to Chapter 3 of the manual for a discussion of score conversions.) Although not intended for routine assessment purposes, subtest scores might be useful for research or highly specialized clinical purposes. If using subtest scores, carefully review Chapter 4 for information about subtest reliability and the reliability of differences between subtests. If the child's *TRI* indicates that he or she may be at risk for atypical development, early intervention and/or further assessment may be necessary.

	Raw Scores	Percentiles	Standard Scores (or T-scores)
Detached			
Hyper-sensitive/active			
Underreactive			
Dysregulated			
Temperament & Regulatory Index (TRI) (total of four factor raw scores)			

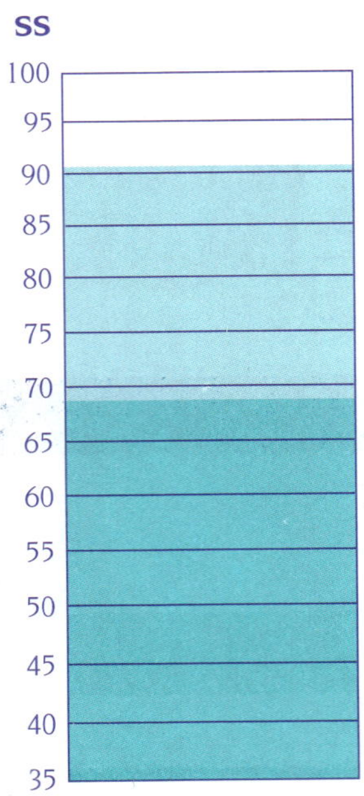

NOTES:

SS = Standard Score (*M* =100, *SD* =15)

☐ Typical ☐ At-Risk ☐ Atypical

 ISBN-13: 978-1-55766-424-2 ISBN-10: 1-55766-424-2
Manufactured in the United States of America.

TABS Assessment Tool

Temperament and Atypical Behavior Scale

Early Childhood Indicators of Developmental Dysfunction

Stephen J. Bagnato, Ed.D., N.C.S.P.
John T. Neisworth, Ph.D.
John Salvia, D.Ed.
Frances M. Hunt, Ph.D.

Instructions for administering the TABS Assessment Tool:

Please refer to Chapter 3 of the **TABS Manual** for important information before administering the TABS Assessment Tool. Complete (or have rater complete) the information in Section I. Read and discuss directions for Section II with the rater, making sure that he or she understands how to respond to the items. Ask the rater to return the Assessment Tool for scoring and interpretation when he or she has completed Section II.

I. CHILD INFORMATION

Name of child: ______________________ Sex: Female ❑ Male ❑

Date of birth: ______________________ Age (in years and months): ______________

Child's address: ______________________

Name of parent or primary caregiver in household: ______________________

Relationship to child: Mother ❑ Father ❑ Other ______________

Telephone number: ______________________ Best time to contact: ______________

List any previously identified problems or diagnoses for this child.

1. ______________________
2. ______________________
3. ______________________

II. TABS INDICATORS

The following 55 items list some of the most frequent problems in temperament and self-regulation that parents and professionals observe in young children. Read each numbered item and check *No* if the behavior is not a problem. Check *Yes* if the behavior is a problem. For those items marked *Yes*, check *Need Help* if there is special concern and assistance is needed to cope with the behavior. Return this form to the individual administering this Assessment Tool for scoring and interpretation.

Name of rater: ______________________ Date Assessment Tool completed: ______________

Relationship to child: ______________________

DETACHED

DETACHED	No	Yes	Need Help
1. Consistently upset by changes in schedule	☐	☐	☐
2. Emotions don't match what is going on	☐	☐	☐
3. Seems to look through or past people	☐	☐	☐
4. Resists looking you in the eye	☐	☐	☐
5. Acts like others are not there	☐	☐	☐
6. Hardly ever starts on own to play with others	☐	☐	☐
7. Moods and wants are too hard to figure out	☐	☐	☐
8. Seems to be in "own world"	☐	☐	☐
9. Often stares into space	☐	☐	☐
10. "Tunes out," loses contact with what is going on	☐	☐	☐
11. Plays with toys in strange ways	☐	☐	☐
12. Plays with toys as if confused by how they work	☐	☐	☐
13. Makes strange throat noises	☐	☐	☐
14. Disturbed by too much light, noise, or touching	☐	☐	☐
15. Overexcited in crowded places	☐	☐	☐
16. Stares at lights	☐	☐	☐
17. Overly interested in toy/object	☐	☐	☐
18. Flaps hands over and over	☐	☐	☐
19. Shakes head over and over	☐	☐	☐
20. Wanders around without purpose	☐	☐	☐

Detached Raw Score → ☐

HYPER-SENSITIVE/ACTIVE

HYPER-SENSITIVE/ACTIVE	No	Yes	Need Help
21. Upset by every little thing	☐	☐	☐
22. Often difficult to soothe when upset and crying	☐	☐	☐
23. Has wide swings in mood	☐	☐	☐
24. Gets angry too easily	☐	☐	☐
25. Too easily frustrated	☐	☐	☐
26. Has wild temper tantrums	☐	☐	☐
27. Frequently irritable, "touchy," or fussy	☐	☐	☐
28. Can't wait at all for food or toy	☐	☐	☐
29. Demands attention continually	☐	☐	☐
30. Controls adult's behavior, "is the boss"	☐	☐	☐

	No	Yes	Need Help
31. Jealous too often	☐	☐	☐
32. Mostly on the go, "in high gear"	☐	☐	☐
33. Doesn't sit still	☐	☐	☐
34. Too "grabby," impulsive	☐	☐	☐
35. Almost always refuses to do what is told	☐	☐	☐
36. Throws or breaks things on purpose	☐	☐	☐
37. Bites, hits, kicks others	☐	☐	☐
Hyper-sensitive/active Raw Score →		☐	

UNDERREACTIVE

	No	Yes	Need Help
38. Rarely smiles, giggles, or laughs at funny things	☐	☐	☐
39. Doesn't pay attention to sights and sounds	☐	☐	☐
40. Doesn't seem to watch moving objects	☐	☐	☐
41. Shows no surprise to new events	☐	☐	☐
42. Doesn't react to own name	☐	☐	☐
43. Doesn't care when others are hurt	☐	☐	☐
44. Doesn't play much at all	☐	☐	☐
45. Doesn't enjoy playing with mother or caregiver	☐	☐	☐
46. Isn't upset when toy is taken away	☐	☐	☐
47. Almost never babbles or tries to talk	☐	☐	☐
48. Doesn't react to sounds	☐	☐	☐
Underreactive Raw Score →		☐	

DYSREGULATED

	No	Yes	Need Help
49. Often cries too long	☐	☐	☐
50. Often frightened by dreams or the nighttime	☐	☐	☐
51. Screams in sleep and can't be comforted	☐	☐	☐
52. Can't comfort self when upset	☐	☐	☐
53. Wakes up often and doesn't fall back asleep	☐	☐	☐
54. Doesn't have a regular sleep schedule	☐	☐	☐
55. Too often needs help to fall asleep	☐	☐	☐
Dysregulated Raw Score →		☐	

III. RESULTS

Add the items marked *Yes* in each of the four subtests, and place the totals in the appropriate boxes marked Raw Score (e.g., *Detached Raw Score*) after each subtest. Transfer those totals to the spaces under the column titled Raw Scores below. Add the four raw scores to calculate the *Temperament & Regulatory Index (TRI)*, and place it in the space provided. Determine percentiles and standard scores (or T-scores) of each of these raw scores by using the Conversion Table in the appendix in the **TABS Manual**. (Refer to Chapter 3 of the manual for a discussion of score conversions.) Although not intended for routine assessment purposes, subtest scores might be useful for research or highly specialized clinical purposes. If using subtest scores, carefully review Chapter 4 for information about subtest reliability and the reliability of differences between subtests. If the child's *TRI* indicates that he or she may be at risk for atypical development, early intervention and/or further assessment may be necessary.

	Raw Scores	Percentiles	Standard Scores (or T-scores)
Detached	....	....	....
Hyper-sensitive/active	....	....	....
Underreactive	....	....	....
Dysregulated	....	....	....
Temperament & Regulatory Index (TRI) (total of four factor raw scores)	________	________	________

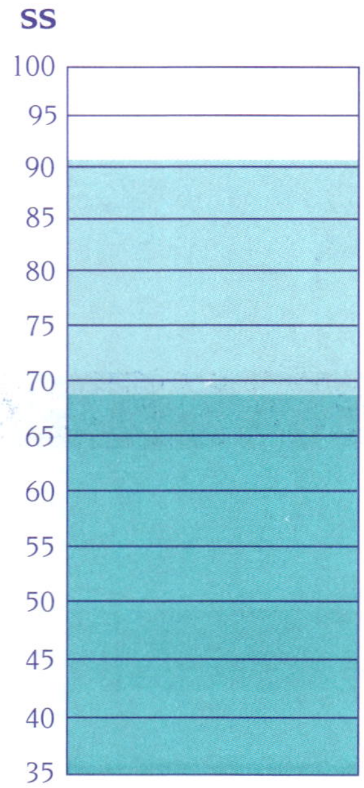

NOTES:

SS = Standard Score (M =100, SD =15)

☐ Typical ☐ At-Risk ☐ Atypical

 ISBN-13: 978-1-55766-424-2 ISBN-10: 1-55766-424-2
Manufactured in the United States of America.

TABS Assessment Tool

Temperament and Atypical Behavior Scale

Early Childhood Indicators of Developmental Dysfunction

Stephen J. Bagnato, Ed.D., N.C.S.P.
John T. Neisworth, Ph.D.
John Salvia, D.Ed.
Frances M. Hunt, Ph.D.

Instructions for administering the TABS Assessment Tool:

Please refer to Chapter 3 of the **TABS Manual** for important information before administering the TABS Assessment Tool. Complete (or have rater complete) the information in Section I. Read and discuss directions for Section II with the rater, making sure that he or she understands how to respond to the items. Ask the rater to return the Assessment Tool for scoring and interpretation when he or she has completed Section II.

I. CHILD INFORMATION

Name of child: ______________________ Sex: Female ❑ Male ❑

Date of birth: ______________________ Age (in years and months): ______________

Child's address: ______________________

Name of parent or primary caregiver in household: ______________________

Relationship to child: Mother ❑ Father ❑ Other ______________________

Telephone number: ______________________ Best time to contact: ______________

List any previously identified problems or diagnoses for this child.

1. ______________________
2. ______________________
3. ______________________

II. TABS INDICATORS

The following 55 items list some of the most frequent problems in temperament and self-regulation that parents and professionals observe in young children. Read each numbered item and check *No* if the behavior is not a problem. Check *Yes* if the behavior is a problem. For those items marked *Yes*, check *Need Help* if there is special concern and assistance is needed to cope with the behavior. Return this form to the individual administering this Assessment Tool for scoring and interpretation.

Name of rater: ______________________ Date Assessment Tool completed: ______________

Relationship to child: ______________________

DETACHED	No	Yes	Need Help
1. Consistently upset by changes in schedule	☐	☐	☐
2. Emotions don't match what is going on	☐	☐	☐
3. Seems to look through or past people	☐	☐	☐
4. Resists looking you in the eye	☐	☐	☐
5. Acts like others are not there	☐	☐	☐
6. Hardly ever starts on own to play with others	☐	☐	☐
7. Moods and wants are too hard to figure out	☐	☐	☐
8. Seems to be in "own world"	☐	☐	☐
9. Often stares into space	☐	☐	☐
10. "Tunes out," loses contact with what is going on	☐	☐	☐
11. Plays with toys in strange ways	☐	☐	☐
12. Plays with toys as if confused by how they work	☐	☐	☐
13. Makes strange throat noises	☐	☐	☐
14. Disturbed by too much light, noise, or touching	☐	☐	☐
15. Overexcited in crowded places	☐	☐	☐
16. Stares at lights	☐	☐	☐
17. Overly interested in toy/object	☐	☐	☐
18. Flaps hands over and over	☐	☐	☐
19. Shakes head over and over	☐	☐	☐
20. Wanders around without purpose	☐	☐	☐
Detached Raw Score →		☐	

HYPER-SENSITIVE/ACTIVE	No	Yes	Need Help
21. Upset by every little thing	☐	☐	☐
22. Often difficult to soothe when upset and crying	☐	☐	☐
23. Has wide swings in mood	☐	☐	☐
24. Gets angry too easily	☐	☐	☐
25. Too easily frustrated	☐	☐	☐
26. Has wild temper tantrums	☐	☐	☐
27. Frequently irritable, "touchy," or fussy	☐	☐	☐
28. Can't wait at all for food or toy	☐	☐	☐
29. Demands attention continually	☐	☐	☐
30. Controls adult's behavior, "is the boss"	☐	☐	☐

	No	Yes	Need Help
31. Jealous too often	☐	☐	☐
32. Mostly on the go, "in high gear"	☐	☐	☐
33. Doesn't sit still	☐	☐	☐
34. Too "grabby," impulsive	☐	☐	☐
35. Almost always refuses to do what is told	☐	☐	☐
36. Throws or breaks things on purpose	☐	☐	☐
37. Bites, hits, kicks others	☐	☐	☐

Hyper-sensitive/active Raw Score → ☐

UNDERREACTIVE

	No	Yes	Need Help
38. Rarely smiles, giggles, or laughs at funny things	☐	☐	☐
39. Doesn't pay attention to sights and sounds	☐	☐	☐
40. Doesn't seem to watch moving objects	☐	☐	☐
41. Shows no surprise to new events	☐	☐	☐
42. Doesn't react to own name	☐	☐	☐
43. Doesn't care when others are hurt	☐	☐	☐
44. Doesn't play much at all	☐	☐	☐
45. Doesn't enjoy playing with mother or caregiver	☐	☐	☐
46. Isn't upset when toy is taken away	☐	☐	☐
47. Almost never babbles or tries to talk	☐	☐	☐
48. Doesn't react to sounds	☐	☐	☐

Underreactive Raw Score → ☐

DYSREGULATED

	No	Yes	Need Help
49. Often cries too long	☐	☐	☐
50. Often frightened by dreams or the nighttime	☐	☐	☐
51. Screams in sleep and can't be comforted	☐	☐	☐
52. Can't comfort self when upset	☐	☐	☐
53. Wakes up often and doesn't fall back asleep	☐	☐	☐
54. Doesn't have a regular sleep schedule	☐	☐	☐
55. Too often needs help to fall asleep	☐	☐	☐

Dysregulated Raw Score → ☐

III. RESULTS

Add the items marked *Yes* in each of the four subtests, and place the totals in the appropriate boxes marked Raw Score (e.g., *Detached Raw Score*) after each subtest. Transfer those totals to the spaces under the column titled Raw Scores below. Add the four raw scores to calculate the *Temperament & Regulatory Index (TRI)*, and place it in the space provided. Determine percentiles and standard scores (or T-scores) of each of these raw scores by using the Conversion Table in the appendix in the **TABS Manual**. (Refer to Chapter 3 of the manual for a discussion of score conversions.) Although not intended for routine assessment purposes, subtest scores might be useful for research or highly specialized clinical purposes. If using subtest scores, carefully review Chapter 4 for information about subtest reliability and the reliability of differences between subtests. If the child's *TRI* indicates that he or she may be at risk for atypical development, early intervention and/or further assessment may be necessary.

	Raw Scores	Percentiles	Standard Scores (or T-scores)
Detached	....	....	....
Hyper-sensitive/active	....	....	....
Underreactive	....	....	....
Dysregulated	....	....	....
Temperament & Regulatory Index (TRI) (total of four factor raw scores)	________	________	________

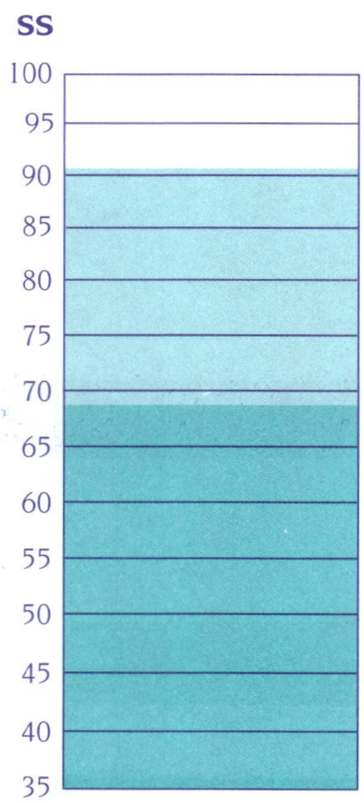

SS = Standard Score (M =100, SD =15)

☐ Typical ☐ At-Risk ☐ Atypical

NOTES:

 ISBN-13: 978-1-55766-424-2 ISBN-10: 1-55766-424-2
Manufactured in the United States of America.

TABS Assessment Tool

Temperament and Atypical Behavior Scale

Early Childhood Indicators of Developmental Dysfunction

Stephen J. Bagnato, Ed.D., N.C.S.P. | John T. Neisworth, Ph.D.
John Salvia, D.Ed. | Frances M. Hunt, Ph.D.

Instructions for administering the TABS Assessment Tool:

Please refer to Chapter 3 of the **TABS Manual** for important information before administering the TABS Assessment Tool. Complete (or have rater complete) the information in Section I. Read and discuss directions for Section II with the rater, making sure that he or she understands how to respond to the items. Ask the rater to return the Assessment Tool for scoring and interpretation when he or she has completed Section II.

I. CHILD INFORMATION

Name of child: ______________________ Sex: Female ❑ Male ❑

Date of birth: ______________________ Age (in years and months): ______________

Child's address: ______________________

Name of parent or primary caregiver in household: ______________________

Relationship to child: Mother ❑ Father ❑ Other ______________________

Telephone number: ______________________ Best time to contact: ______________

List any previously identified problems or diagnoses for this child.

1. ______________________
2. ______________________
3. ______________________

II. TABS INDICATORS

The following 55 items list some of the most frequent problems in temperament and self-regulation that parents and professionals observe in young children. Read each numbered item and check *No* if the behavior is not a problem. Check *Yes* if the behavior is a problem. For those items marked *Yes*, check *Need Help* if there is special concern and assistance is needed to cope with the behavior. Return this form to the individual administering this Assessment Tool for scoring and interpretation.

Name of rater: ______________________ Date Assessment Tool completed: ______________

Relationship to child: ______________________

DETACHED	No	Yes	Need Help
1. Consistently upset by changes in schedule	☐	☐	☐
2. Emotions don't match what is going on	☐	☐	☐
3. Seems to look through or past people	☐	☐	☐
4. Resists looking you in the eye	☐	☐	☐
5. Acts like others are not there	☐	☐	☐
6. Hardly ever starts on own to play with others	☐	☐	☐
7. Moods and wants are too hard to figure out	☐	☐	☐
8. Seems to be in "own world"	☐	☐	☐
9. Often stares into space	☐	☐	☐
10. "Tunes out," loses contact with what is going on	☐	☐	☐
11. Plays with toys in strange ways	☐	☐	☐
12. Plays with toys as if confused by how they work	☐	☐	☐
13. Makes strange throat noises	☐	☐	☐
14. Disturbed by too much light, noise, or touching	☐	☐	☐
15. Overexcited in crowded places	☐	☐	☐
16. Stares at lights	☐	☐	☐
17. Overly interested in toy/object	☐	☐	☐
18. Flaps hands over and over	☐	☐	☐
19. Shakes head over and over	☐	☐	☐
20. Wanders around without purpose	☐	☐	☐
Detached Raw Score →		☐	

HYPER-SENSITIVE/ACTIVE	No	Yes	Need Help
21. Upset by every little thing	☐	☐	☐
22. Often difficult to soothe when upset and crying	☐	☐	☐
23. Has wide swings in mood	☐	☐	☐
24. Gets angry too easily	☐	☐	☐
25. Too easily frustrated	☐	☐	☐
26. Has wild temper tantrums	☐	☐	☐
27. Frequently irritable, "touchy," or fussy	☐	☐	☐
28. Can't wait at all for food or toy	☐	☐	☐
29. Demands attention continually	☐	☐	☐
30. Controls adult's behavior, "is the boss"	☐	☐	☐

	No	Yes	Need Help
31. Jealous too often	☐	☐	☐
32. Mostly on the go, "in high gear"	☐	☐	☐
33. Doesn't sit still	☐	☐	☐
34. Too "grabby," impulsive	☐	☐	☐
35. Almost always refuses to do what is told	☐	☐	☐
36. Throws or breaks things on purpose	☐	☐	☐
37. Bites, hits, kicks others	☐	☐	☐

Hyper-sensitive/active Raw Score → ☐

UNDERREACTIVE

	No	Yes	Need Help
38. Rarely smiles, giggles, or laughs at funny things	☐	☐	☐
39. Doesn't pay attention to sights and sounds	☐	☐	☐
40. Doesn't seem to watch moving objects	☐	☐	☐
41. Shows no surprise to new events	☐	☐	☐
42. Doesn't react to own name	☐	☐	☐
43. Doesn't care when others are hurt	☐	☐	☐
44. Doesn't play much at all	☐	☐	☐
45. Doesn't enjoy playing with mother or caregiver	☐	☐	☐
46. Isn't upset when toy is taken away	☐	☐	☐
47. Almost never babbles or tries to talk	☐	☐	☐
48. Doesn't react to sounds	☐	☐	☐

Underreactive Raw Score → ☐

DYSREGULATED

	No	Yes	Need Help
49. Often cries too long	☐	☐	☐
50. Often frightened by dreams or the nighttime	☐	☐	☐
51. Screams in sleep and can't be comforted	☐	☐	☐
52. Can't comfort self when upset	☐	☐	☐
53. Wakes up often and doesn't fall back asleep	☐	☐	☐
54. Doesn't have a regular sleep schedule	☐	☐	☐
55. Too often needs help to fall asleep	☐	☐	☐

Dysregulated Raw Score → ☐

III. RESULTS

Add the items marked *Yes* in each of the four subtests, and place the totals in the appropriate boxes marked Raw Score (e.g., *Detached Raw Score*) after each subtest. Transfer those totals to the spaces under the column titled Raw Scores below. Add the four raw scores to calculate the *Temperament & Regulatory Index (TRI),* and place it in the space provided. Determine percentiles and standard scores (or T-scores) of each of these raw scores by using the Conversion Table in the appendix in the **TABS Manual**. (Refer to Chapter 3 of the manual for a discussion of score conversions.) Although not intended for routine assessment purposes, subtest scores might be useful for research or highly specialized clinical purposes. If using subtest scores, carefully review Chapter 4 for information about subtest reliability and the reliability of differences between subtests. If the child's *TRI* indicates that he or she may be at risk for atypical development, early intervention and/or further assessment may be necessary.

	Raw Scores	Percentiles	Standard Scores (or T-scores)
Detached			
Hyper-sensitive/active			
Underreactive			
Dysregulated			
Temperament & Regulatory Index (TRI) (total of four factor raw scores)			

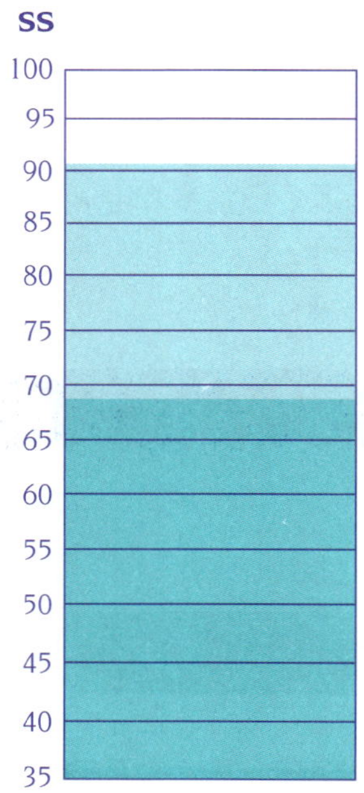

NOTES:

SS = Standard Score (*M* =100, *SD* =15)

Typical At-Risk Atypical

 ISBN-13: 978-1-55766-424-2 ISBN-10: 1-55766-424-2
Manufactured in the United States of America.

TABS Assessment Tool

Temperament and Atypical Behavior Scale

Early Childhood Indicators of Developmental Dysfunction

Stephen J. Bagnato, Ed.D., N.C.S.P.
John T. Neisworth, Ph.D.
John Salvia, D.Ed.
Frances M. Hunt, Ph.D.

Instructions for administering the TABS Assessment Tool:

Please refer to Chapter 3 of the **TABS Manual** for important information before administering the TABS Assessment Tool. Complete (or have rater complete) the information in Section I. Read and discuss directions for Section II with the rater, making sure that he or she understands how to respond to the items. Ask the rater to return the Assessment Tool for scoring and interpretation when he or she has completed Section II.

I. CHILD INFORMATION

Name of child: ______________________ Sex: Female ❑ Male ❑

Date of birth: ______________________ Age (in years and months): ______________

Child's address: ______________________

Name of parent or primary caregiver in household: ______________________

Relationship to child: Mother ❑ Father ❑ Other ______________________

Telephone number: ______________________ Best time to contact: ______________

List any previously identified problems or diagnoses for this child.

1. ______________________
2. ______________________
3. ______________________

II. TABS INDICATORS

The following 55 items list some of the most frequent problems in temperament and self-regulation that parents and professionals observe in young children. Read each numbered item and check *No* if the behavior is not a problem. Check *Yes* if the behavior is a problem. For those items marked *Yes*, check *Need Help* if there is special concern and assistance is needed to cope with the behavior. Return this form to the individual administering this Assessment Tool for scoring and interpretation.

Name of rater: ______________________ Date Assessment Tool completed: ______________

Relationship to child: ______________________

1-800-638-3775 www.brookespublishing.com

DETACHED	No	Yes	Need Help
1. Consistently upset by changes in schedule	☐	☐	☐
2. Emotions don't match what is going on	☐	☐	☐
3. Seems to look through or past people	☐	☐	☐
4. Resists looking you in the eye	☐	☐	☐
5. Acts like others are not there	☐	☐	☐
6. Hardly ever starts on own to play with others	☐	☐	☐
7. Moods and wants are too hard to figure out	☐	☐	☐
8. Seems to be in "own world"	☐	☐	☐
9. Often stares into space	☐	☐	☐
10. "Tunes out," loses contact with what is going on	☐	☐	☐
11. Plays with toys in strange ways	☐	☐	☐
12. Plays with toys as if confused by how they work	☐	☐	☐
13. Makes strange throat noises	☐	☐	☐
14. Disturbed by too much light, noise, or touching	☐	☐	☐
15. Overexcited in crowded places	☐	☐	☐
16. Stares at lights	☐	☐	☐
17. Overly interested in toy/object	☐	☐	☐
18. Flaps hands over and over	☐	☐	☐
19. Shakes head over and over	☐	☐	☐
20. Wanders around without purpose	☐	☐	☐
Detached Raw Score →		☐	

HYPER-SENSITIVE/ACTIVE	No	Yes	Need Help
21. Upset by every little thing	☐	☐	☐
22. Often difficult to soothe when upset and crying	☐	☐	☐
23. Has wide swings in mood	☐	☐	☐
24. Gets angry too easily	☐	☐	☐
25. Too easily frustrated	☐	☐	☐
26. Has wild temper tantrums	☐	☐	☐
27. Frequently irritable, "touchy," or fussy	☐	☐	☐
28. Can't wait at all for food or toy	☐	☐	☐
29. Demands attention continually	☐	☐	☐
30. Controls adult's behavior, "is the boss"	☐	☐	☐

	No	Yes	Need Help
31. Jealous too often	☐	☐	☐
32. Mostly on the go, "in high gear"	☐	☐	☐
33. Doesn't sit still	☐	☐	☐
34. Too "grabby," impulsive	☐	☐	☐
35. Almost always refuses to do what is told	☐	☐	☐
36. Throws or breaks things on purpose	☐	☐	☐
37. Bites, hits, kicks others	☐	☐	☐
Hyper-sensitive/active Raw Score →		☐	

UNDERREACTIVE

	No	Yes	Need Help
38. Rarely smiles, giggles, or laughs at funny things	☐	☐	☐
39. Doesn't pay attention to sights and sounds	☐	☐	☐
40. Doesn't seem to watch moving objects	☐	☐	☐
41. Shows no surprise to new events	☐	☐	☐
42. Doesn't react to own name	☐	☐	☐
43. Doesn't care when others are hurt	☐	☐	☐
44. Doesn't play much at all	☐	☐	☐
45. Doesn't enjoy playing with mother or caregiver	☐	☐	☐
46. Isn't upset when toy is taken away	☐	☐	☐
47. Almost never babbles or tries to talk	☐	☐	☐
48. Doesn't react to sounds	☐	☐	☐
Underreactive Raw Score →		☐	

DYSREGULATED

	No	Yes	Need Help
49. Often cries too long	☐	☐	☐
50. Often frightened by dreams or the nighttime	☐	☐	☐
51. Screams in sleep and can't be comforted	☐	☐	☐
52. Can't comfort self when upset	☐	☐	☐
53. Wakes up often and doesn't fall back asleep	☐	☐	☐
54. Doesn't have a regular sleep schedule	☐	☐	☐
55. Too often needs help to fall asleep	☐	☐	☐
Dysregulated Raw Score →		☐	

III. RESULTS

Add the items marked *Yes* in each of the four subtests, and place the totals in the appropriate boxes marked Raw Score (e.g., *Detached Raw Score*) after each subtest. Transfer those totals to the spaces under the column titled Raw Scores below. Add the four raw scores to calculate the *Temperament & Regulatory Index (TRI),* and place it in the space provided. Determine percentiles and standard scores (or T-scores) of each of these raw scores by using the Conversion Table in the appendix in the **TABS Manual**. (Refer to Chapter 3 of the manual for a discussion of score conversions.) Although not intended for routine assessment purposes, subtest scores might be useful for research or highly specialized clinical purposes. If using subtest scores, carefully review Chapter 4 for information about subtest reliability and the reliability of differences between subtests. If the child's *TRI* indicates that he or she may be at risk for atypical development, early intervention and/or further assessment may be necessary.

	Raw Scores	Percentiles	Standard Scores (or T-scores)
Detached			
Hyper-sensitive/active			
Underreactive			
Dysregulated			
Temperament & Regulatory Index (TRI) (total of four factor raw scores)			

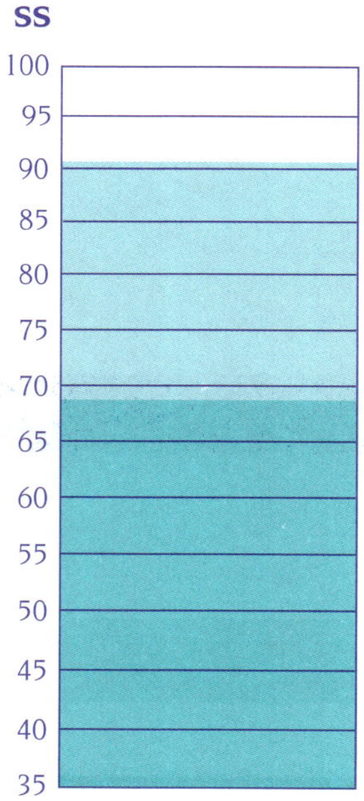

NOTES:

SS = Standard Score (*M* =100, *SD* =15)

Typical At-Risk Atypical

 ISBN-13: 978-1-55766-424-2 ISBN-10: 1-55766-424-2
Manufactured in the United States of America.

TABS Assessment Tool

Temperament and Atypical Behavior Scale

Early Childhood Indicators of Developmental Dysfunction

Stephen J. Bagnato, Ed.D., N.C.S.P. | John T. Neisworth, Ph.D.

John Salvia, D.Ed. | Frances M. Hunt, Ph.D.

Instructions for administering the TABS Assessment Tool:

Please refer to Chapter 3 of the **TABS Manual** for important information before administering the TABS Assessment Tool. Complete (or have rater complete) the information in Section I. Read and discuss directions for Section II with the rater, making sure that he or she understands how to respond to the items. Ask the rater to return the Assessment Tool for scoring and interpretation when he or she has completed Section II.

I. CHILD INFORMATION

Name of child: ______________________ Sex: Female ❑ Male ❑

Date of birth: ______________________ Age (in years and months): ______________________

Child's address: ______________________

Name of parent or primary caregiver in household: ______________________

Relationship to child: Mother ❑ Father ❑ Other ______________________

Telephone number: ______________________ Best time to contact: ______________________

List any previously identified problems or diagnoses for this child.

1. ______________________
2. ______________________
3. ______________________

II. TABS INDICATORS

The following 55 items list some of the most frequent problems in temperament and self-regulation that parents and professionals observe in young children. Read each numbered item and check *No* if the behavior is not a problem. Check *Yes* if the behavior is a problem. For those items marked *Yes*, check *Need Help* if there is special concern and assistance is needed to cope with the behavior. Return this form to the individual administering this Assessment Tool for scoring and interpretation.

Name of rater: ______________________ Date Assessment Tool completed: ______________________

Relationship to child: ______________________

1-800-638-3775 www.brookespublishing.com

DETACHED

	No	Yes	Need Help
1. Consistently upset by changes in schedule	☐	☐	☐
2. Emotions don't match what is going on	☐	☐	☐
3. Seems to look through or past people	☐	☐	☐
4. Resists looking you in the eye	☐	☐	☐
5. Acts like others are not there	☐	☐	☐
6. Hardly ever starts on own to play with others	☐	☐	☐
7. Moods and wants are too hard to figure out	☐	☐	☐
8. Seems to be in "own world"	☐	☐	☐
9. Often stares into space	☐	☐	☐
10. "Tunes out," loses contact with what is going on	☐	☐	☐
11. Plays with toys in strange ways	☐	☐	☐
12. Plays with toys as if confused by how they work	☐	☐	☐
13. Makes strange throat noises	☐	☐	☐
14. Disturbed by too much light, noise, or touching	☐	☐	☐
15. Overexcited in crowded places	☐	☐	☐
16. Stares at lights	☐	☐	☐
17. Overly interested in toy/object	☐	☐	☐
18. Flaps hands over and over	☐	☐	☐
19. Shakes head over and over	☐	☐	☐
20. Wanders around without purpose	☐	☐	☐

Detached Raw Score → ☐

HYPER-SENSITIVE/ACTIVE

	No	Yes	Need Help
21. Upset by every little thing	☐	☐	☐
22. Often difficult to soothe when upset and crying	☐	☐	☐
23. Has wide swings in mood	☐	☐	☐
24. Gets angry too easily	☐	☐	☐
25. Too easily frustrated	☐	☐	☐
26. Has wild temper tantrums	☐	☐	☐
27. Frequently irritable, "touchy," or fussy	☐	☐	☐
28. Can't wait at all for food or toy	☐	☐	☐
29. Demands attention continually	☐	☐	☐
30. Controls adult's behavior, "is the boss"	☐	☐	☐

	No	Yes	Need Help
31. Jealous too often	☐	☐	☐
32. Mostly on the go, "in high gear"	☐	☐	☐
33. Doesn't sit still	☐	☐	☐
34. Too "grabby," impulsive	☐	☐	☐
35. Almost always refuses to do what is told	☐	☐	☐
36. Throws or breaks things on purpose	☐	☐	☐
37. Bites, hits, kicks others	☐	☐	☐
Hyper-sensitive/active Raw Score →		☐	

UNDERREACTIVE

	No	Yes	Need Help
38. Rarely smiles, giggles, or laughs at funny things	☐	☐	☐
39. Doesn't pay attention to sights and sounds	☐	☐	☐
40. Doesn't seem to watch moving objects	☐	☐	☐
41. Shows no surprise to new events	☐	☐	☐
42. Doesn't react to own name	☐	☐	☐
43. Doesn't care when others are hurt	☐	☐	☐
44. Doesn't play much at all	☐	☐	☐
45. Doesn't enjoy playing with mother or caregiver	☐	☐	☐
46. Isn't upset when toy is taken away	☐	☐	☐
47. Almost never babbles or tries to talk	☐	☐	☐
48. Doesn't react to sounds	☐	☐	☐
Underreactive Raw Score →		☐	

DYSREGULATED

	No	Yes	Need Help
49. Often cries too long	☐	☐	☐
50. Often frightened by dreams or the nighttime	☐	☐	☐
51. Screams in sleep and can't be comforted	☐	☐	☐
52. Can't comfort self when upset	☐	☐	☐
53. Wakes up often and doesn't fall back asleep	☐	☐	☐
54. Doesn't have a regular sleep schedule	☐	☐	☐
55. Too often needs help to fall asleep	☐	☐	☐
Dysregulated Raw Score →		☐	

III. RESULTS

Add the items marked *Yes* in each of the four subtests, and place the totals in the appropriate boxes marked Raw Score (e.g., *Detached Raw Score*) after each subtest. Transfer those totals to the spaces under the column titled Raw Scores below. Add the four raw scores to calculate the *Temperament & Regulatory Index (TRI),* and place it in the space provided. Determine percentiles and standard scores (or T-scores) of each of these raw scores by using the Conversion Table in the appendix in the **TABS Manual**. (Refer to Chapter 3 of the manual for a discussion of score conversions.) Although not intended for routine assessment purposes, subtest scores might be useful for research or highly specialized clinical purposes. If using subtest scores, carefully review Chapter 4 for information about subtest reliability and the reliability of differences between subtests. If the child's *TRI* indicates that he or she may be at risk for atypical development, early intervention and/or further assessment may be necessary.

	Raw Scores	Percentiles	Standard Scores (or T-scores)
Detached	....	....	....
Hyper-sensitive/active	....	....	....
Underreactive	....	....	....
Dysregulated	....	....	....
Temperament & Regulatory Index (TRI) (total of four factor raw scores)	________	________	________

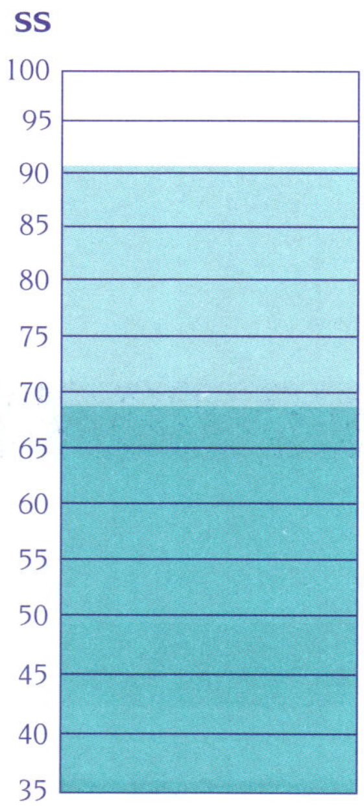

NOTES:

SS = Standard Score (*M* =100, *SD* =15)

☐ Typical ☐ At-Risk ☐ Atypical

 ISBN-13: 978-1-55766-424-2 ISBN-10: 1-55766-424-2
Manufactured in the United States of America.

TABS Assessment Tool

Temperament and Atypical Behavior Scale

Early Childhood Indicators of Developmental Dysfunction

Stephen J. Bagnato, Ed.D., N.C.S.P. | John T. Neisworth, Ph.D.

John Salvia, D.Ed. | Frances M. Hunt, Ph.D.

Instructions for administering the TABS Assessment Tool:

Please refer to Chapter 3 of the **TABS Manual** for important information before administering the TABS Assessment Tool. Complete (or have rater complete) the information in Section I. Read and discuss directions for Section II with the rater, making sure that he or she understands how to respond to the items. Ask the rater to return the Assessment Tool for scoring and interpretation when he or she has completed Section II.

I. CHILD INFORMATION

Name of child: ______________________ Sex: Female ❑ Male ❑

Date of birth: ______________________ Age (in years and months): ______________

Child's address: ______________________

Name of parent or primary caregiver in household: ______________________

Relationship to child: Mother ❑ Father ❑ Other ______________________

Telephone number: ______________________ Best time to contact: ______________

List any previously identified problems or diagnoses for this child.

1. ______________________
2. ______________________
3. ______________________

II. TABS INDICATORS

The following 55 items list some of the most frequent problems in temperament and self-regulation that parents and professionals observe in young children. Read each numbered item and check *No* if the behavior is not a problem. Check *Yes* if the behavior is a problem. For those items marked *Yes*, check *Need Help* if there is special concern and assistance is needed to cope with the behavior. Return this form to the individual administering this Assessment Tool for scoring and interpretation.

Name of rater: ______________________ Date Assessment Tool completed: ______________

Relationship to child: ______________________

1-800-638-3775 www.brookespublishing.com

DETACHED

DETACHED	No	Yes	Need Help
1. Consistently upset by changes in schedule	☐	☐	☐
2. Emotions don't match what is going on	☐	☐	☐
3. Seems to look through or past people	☐	☐	☐
4. Resists looking you in the eye	☐	☐	☐
5. Acts like others are not there	☐	☐	☐
6. Hardly ever starts on own to play with others	☐	☐	☐
7. Moods and wants are too hard to figure out	☐	☐	☐
8. Seems to be in "own world"	☐	☐	☐
9. Often stares into space	☐	☐	☐
10. "Tunes out," loses contact with what is going on	☐	☐	☐
11. Plays with toys in strange ways	☐	☐	☐
12. Plays with toys as if confused by how they work	☐	☐	☐
13. Makes strange throat noises	☐	☐	☐
14. Disturbed by too much light, noise, or touching	☐	☐	☐
15. Overexcited in crowded places	☐	☐	☐
16. Stares at lights	☐	☐	☐
17. Overly interested in toy/object	☐	☐	☐
18. Flaps hands over and over	☐	☐	☐
19. Shakes head over and over	☐	☐	☐
20. Wanders around without purpose	☐	☐	☐

Detached Raw Score → ☐

HYPER-SENSITIVE/ACTIVE

HYPER-SENSITIVE/ACTIVE	No	Yes	Need Help
21. Upset by every little thing	☐	☐	☐
22. Often difficult to soothe when upset and crying	☐	☐	☐
23. Has wide swings in mood	☐	☐	☐
24. Gets angry too easily	☐	☐	☐
25. Too easily frustrated	☐	☐	☐
26. Has wild temper tantrums	☐	☐	☐
27. Frequently irritable, "touchy," or fussy	☐	☐	☐
28. Can't wait at all for food or toy	☐	☐	☐
29. Demands attention continually	☐	☐	☐
30. Controls adult's behavior, "is the boss"	☐	☐	☐

	No	Yes	Need Help
31. Jealous too often	☐	☐	☐
32. Mostly on the go, "in high gear"	☐	☐	☐
33. Doesn't sit still	☐	☐	☐
34. Too "grabby," impulsive	☐	☐	☐
35. Almost always refuses to do what is told	☐	☐	☐
36. Throws or breaks things on purpose	☐	☐	☐
37. Bites, hits, kicks others	☐	☐	☐
Hyper-sensitive/active Raw Score →		☐	

UNDERREACTIVE

	No	Yes	Need Help
38. Rarely smiles, giggles, or laughs at funny things	☐	☐	☐
39. Doesn't pay attention to sights and sounds	☐	☐	☐
40. Doesn't seem to watch moving objects	☐	☐	☐
41. Shows no surprise to new events	☐	☐	☐
42. Doesn't react to own name	☐	☐	☐
43. Doesn't care when others are hurt	☐	☐	☐
44. Doesn't play much at all	☐	☐	☐
45. Doesn't enjoy playing with mother or caregiver	☐	☐	☐
46. Isn't upset when toy is taken away	☐	☐	☐
47. Almost never babbles or tries to talk	☐	☐	☐
48. Doesn't react to sounds	☐	☐	☐
Underreactive Raw Score →		☐	

DYSREGULATED

	No	Yes	Need Help
49. Often cries too long	☐	☐	☐
50. Often frightened by dreams or the nighttime	☐	☐	☐
51. Screams in sleep and can't be comforted	☐	☐	☐
52. Can't comfort self when upset	☐	☐	☐
53. Wakes up often and doesn't fall back asleep	☐	☐	☐
54. Doesn't have a regular sleep schedule	☐	☐	☐
55. Too often needs help to fall asleep	☐	☐	☐
Dysregulated Raw Score →		☐	

III. RESULTS

Add the items marked *Yes* in each of the four subtests, and place the totals in the appropriate boxes marked Raw Score (e.g., *Detached Raw Score*) after each subtest. Transfer those totals to the spaces under the column titled Raw Scores below. Add the four raw scores to calculate the *Temperament & Regulatory Index (TRI)*, and place it in the space provided. Determine percentiles and standard scores (or T-scores) of each of these raw scores by using the Conversion Table in the appendix in the **TABS Manual**. (Refer to Chapter 3 of the manual for a discussion of score conversions.) Although not intended for routine assessment purposes, subtest scores might be useful for research or highly specialized clinical purposes. If using subtest scores, carefully review Chapter 4 for information about subtest reliability and the reliability of differences between subtests. If the child's *TRI* indicates that he or she may be at risk for atypical development, early intervention and/or further assessment may be necessary.

	Raw Scores	Percentiles	Standard Scores (or T-scores)
Detached			
Hyper-sensitive/active			
Underreactive			
Dysregulated			
Temperament & Regulatory Index (TRI) (total of four factor raw scores)			

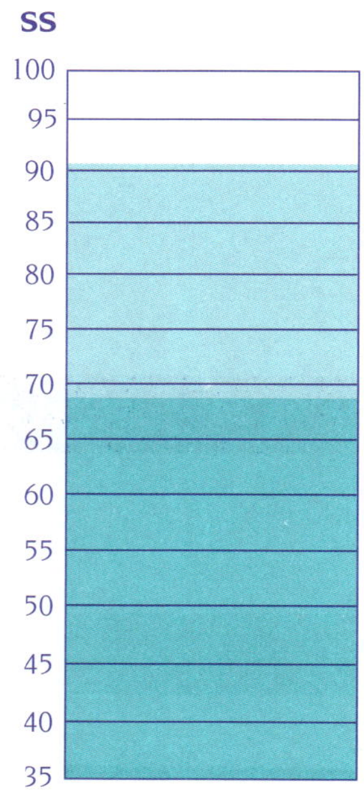

NOTES:

SS = Standard Score (M =100, SD =15)

Typical At-Risk Atypical

 ISBN-13: 978-1-55766-424-2 ISBN-10: 1-55766-424-2
Manufactured in the United States of America.

TABS Assessment Tool

Temperament and Atypical Behavior Scale

Early Childhood Indicators of Developmental Dysfunction

Stephen J. Bagnato, Ed.D., N.C.S.P. | John T. Neisworth, Ph.D.
John Salvia, D.Ed. | Frances M. Hunt, Ph.D.

Instructions for administering the TABS Assessment Tool:

Please refer to Chapter 3 of the **TABS Manual** for important information before administering the TABS Assessment Tool. Complete (or have rater complete) the information in Section I. Read and discuss directions for Section II with the rater, making sure that he or she understands how to respond to the items. Ask the rater to return the Assessment Tool for scoring and interpretation when he or she has completed Section II.

I. CHILD INFORMATION

Name of child: ______________________ Sex: Female ❑ Male ❑

Date of birth: ______________________ Age (in years and months): ______________________

Child's address: ______________________

Name of parent or primary caregiver in household: ______________________

Relationship to child: Mother ❑ Father ❑ Other ______________________

Telephone number: ______________________ Best time to contact: ______________________

List any previously identified problems or diagnoses for this child.

1. ______________________
2. ______________________
3. ______________________

II. TABS INDICATORS

The following 55 items list some of the most frequent problems in temperament and self-regulation that parents and professionals observe in young children. Read each numbered item and check *No* if the behavior is not a problem. Check *Yes* if the behavior is a problem. For those items marked *Yes*, check *Need Help* if there is special concern and assistance is needed to cope with the behavior. Return this form to the individual administering this Assessment Tool for scoring and interpretation.

Name of rater: ______________________ Date Assessment Tool completed: ______________________

Relationship to child: ______________________

DETACHED	No	Yes	Need Help
1. Consistently upset by changes in schedule	☐	☐	☐
2. Emotions don't match what is going on	☐	☐	☐
3. Seems to look through or past people	☐	☐	☐
4. Resists looking you in the eye	☐	☐	☐
5. Acts like others are not there	☐	☐	☐
6. Hardly ever starts on own to play with others	☐	☐	☐
7. Moods and wants are too hard to figure out	☐	☐	☐
8. Seems to be in "own world"	☐	☐	☐
9. Often stares into space	☐	☐	☐
10. "Tunes out," loses contact with what is going on	☐	☐	☐
11. Plays with toys in strange ways	☐	☐	☐
12. Plays with toys as if confused by how they work	☐	☐	☐
13. Makes strange throat noises	☐	☐	☐
14. Disturbed by too much light, noise, or touching	☐	☐	☐
15. Overexcited in crowded places	☐	☐	☐
16. Stares at lights	☐	☐	☐
17. Overly interested in toy/object	☐	☐	☐
18. Flaps hands over and over	☐	☐	☐
19. Shakes head over and over	☐	☐	☐
20. Wanders around without purpose	☐	☐	☐
Detached Raw Score →		☐	

HYPER-SENSITIVE/ACTIVE	No	Yes	Need Help
21. Upset by every little thing	☐	☐	☐
22. Often difficult to soothe when upset and crying	☐	☐	☐
23. Has wide swings in mood	☐	☐	☐
24. Gets angry too easily	☐	☐	☐
25. Too easily frustrated	☐	☐	☐
26. Has wild temper tantrums	☐	☐	☐
27. Frequently irritable, "touchy," or fussy	☐	☐	☐
28. Can't wait at all for food or toy	☐	☐	☐
29. Demands attention continually	☐	☐	☐
30. Controls adult's behavior, "is the boss"	☐	☐	☐

	No	Yes	Need Help
31. Jealous too often	☐	☐	☐
32. Mostly on the go, "in high gear"	☐	☐	☐
33. Doesn't sit still	☐	☐	☐
34. Too "grabby," impulsive	☐	☐	☐
35. Almost always refuses to do what is told	☐	☐	☐
36. Throws or breaks things on purpose	☐	☐	☐
37. Bites, hits, kicks others	☐	☐	☐

Hyper-sensitive/active Raw Score → ☐

UNDERREACTIVE

	No	Yes	Need Help
38. Rarely smiles, giggles, or laughs at funny things	☐	☐	☐
39. Doesn't pay attention to sights and sounds	☐	☐	☐
40. Doesn't seem to watch moving objects	☐	☐	☐
41. Shows no surprise to new events	☐	☐	☐
42. Doesn't react to own name	☐	☐	☐
43. Doesn't care when others are hurt	☐	☐	☐
44. Doesn't play much at all	☐	☐	☐
45. Doesn't enjoy playing with mother or caregiver	☐	☐	☐
46. Isn't upset when toy is taken away	☐	☐	☐
47. Almost never babbles or tries to talk	☐	☐	☐
48. Doesn't react to sounds	☐	☐	☐

Underreactive Raw Score → ☐

DYSREGULATED

	No	Yes	Need Help
49. Often cries too long	☐	☐	☐
50. Often frightened by dreams or the nighttime	☐	☐	☐
51. Screams in sleep and can't be comforted	☐	☐	☐
52. Can't comfort self when upset	☐	☐	☐
53. Wakes up often and doesn't fall back asleep	☐	☐	☐
54. Doesn't have a regular sleep schedule	☐	☐	☐
55. Too often needs help to fall asleep	☐	☐	☐

Dysregulated Raw Score → ☐

III. RESULTS

Add the items marked *Yes* in each of the four subtests, and place the totals in the appropriate boxes marked Raw Score (e.g., *Detached Raw Score*) after each subtest. Transfer those totals to the spaces under the column titled Raw Scores below. Add the four raw scores to calculate the *Temperament & Regulatory Index (TRI)*, and place it in the space provided. Determine percentiles and standard scores (or T-scores) of each of these raw scores by using the Conversion Table in the appendix in the **TABS Manual**. (Refer to Chapter 3 of the manual for a discussion of score conversions.) Although not intended for routine assessment purposes, subtest scores might be useful for research or highly specialized clinical purposes. If using subtest scores, carefully review Chapter 4 for information about subtest reliability and the reliability of differences between subtests. If the child's *TRI* indicates that he or she may be at risk for atypical development, early intervention and/or further assessment may be necessary.

	Raw Scores	Percentiles	Standard Scores (or T-scores)
Detached	....	....	....
Hyper-sensitive/active	....	....	....
Underreactive	....	....	....
Dysregulated	....	....	....
Temperament & Regulatory Index (TRI) (total of four factor raw scores)	______	______	______

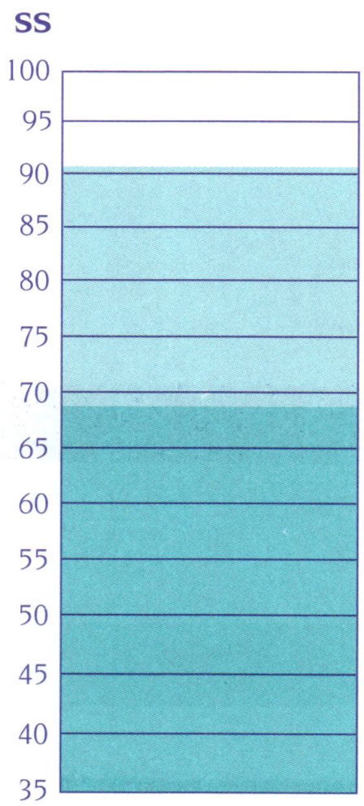

NOTES:

SS = Standard Score (M =100, SD =15)

☐ Typical ☐ At-Risk ☐ Atypical

 ISBN-13: 978-1-55766-424-2 ISBN-10: 1-55766-424-2
Manufactured in the United States of America.

TABS Assessment Tool

Temperament and Atypical Behavior Scale

Early Childhood Indicators of Developmental Dysfunction

Stephen J. Bagnato, Ed.D., N.C.S.P.
John T. Neisworth, Ph.D.
John Salvia, D.Ed.
Frances M. Hunt, Ph.D.

Instructions for administering the TABS Assessment Tool:

Please refer to Chapter 3 of the **TABS Manual** for important information before administering the TABS Assessment Tool. Complete (or have rater complete) the information in Section I. Read and discuss directions for Section II with the rater, making sure that he or she understands how to respond to the items. Ask the rater to return the Assessment Tool for scoring and interpretation when he or she has completed Section II.

I. CHILD INFORMATION

Name of child: ______________________ Sex: Female ❑ Male ❑

Date of birth: ______________________ Age (in years and months): ______________

Child's address: ______________________

Name of parent or primary caregiver in household: ______________________

Relationship to child: Mother ❑ Father ❑ Other ______________________

Telephone number: ______________________ Best time to contact: ______________

List any previously identified problems or diagnoses for this child.

1. ______________________
2. ______________________
3. ______________________

II. TABS INDICATORS

The following 55 items list some of the most frequent problems in temperament and self-regulation that parents and professionals observe in young children. Read each numbered item and check *No* if the behavior is not a problem. Check *Yes* if the behavior is a problem. For those items marked *Yes*, check *Need Help* if there is special concern and assistance is needed to cope with the behavior. Return this form to the individual administering this Assessment Tool for scoring and interpretation.

Name of rater: ______________________ Date Assessment Tool completed: ______________

Relationship to child: ______________________

DETACHED	No	Yes	Need Help
1. Consistently upset by changes in schedule	☐	☐	☐
2. Emotions don't match what is going on	☐	☐	☐
3. Seems to look through or past people	☐	☐	☐
4. Resists looking you in the eye	☐	☐	☐
5. Acts like others are not there	☐	☐	☐
6. Hardly ever starts on own to play with others	☐	☐	☐
7. Moods and wants are too hard to figure out	☐	☐	☐
8. Seems to be in "own world"	☐	☐	☐
9. Often stares into space	☐	☐	☐
10. "Tunes out," loses contact with what is going on	☐	☐	☐
11. Plays with toys in strange ways	☐	☐	☐
12. Plays with toys as if confused by how they work	☐	☐	☐
13. Makes strange throat noises	☐	☐	☐
14. Disturbed by too much light, noise, or touching	☐	☐	☐
15. Overexcited in crowded places	☐	☐	☐
16. Stares at lights	☐	☐	☐
17. Overly interested in toy/object	☐	☐	☐
18. Flaps hands over and over	☐	☐	☐
19. Shakes head over and over	☐	☐	☐
20. Wanders around without purpose	☐	☐	☐
Detached Raw Score →		☐	

HYPER-SENSITIVE/ACTIVE	No	Yes	Need Help
21. Upset by every little thing	☐	☐	☐
22. Often difficult to soothe when upset and crying	☐	☐	☐
23. Has wide swings in mood	☐	☐	☐
24. Gets angry too easily	☐	☐	☐
25. Too easily frustrated	☐	☐	☐
26. Has wild temper tantrums	☐	☐	☐
27. Frequently irritable, "touchy," or fussy	☐	☐	☐
28. Can't wait at all for food or toy	☐	☐	☐
29. Demands attention continually	☐	☐	☐
30. Controls adult's behavior, "is the boss"	☐	☐	☐

	No	Yes	Need Help
31. Jealous too often	☐	☐	☐
32. Mostly on the go, "in high gear"	☐	☐	☐
33. Doesn't sit still	☐	☐	☐
34. Too "grabby," impulsive	☐	☐	☐
35. Almost always refuses to do what is told	☐	☐	☐
36. Throws or breaks things on purpose	☐	☐	☐
37. Bites, hits, kicks others	☐	☐	☐

Hyper-sensitive/active Raw Score → ☐

UNDERREACTIVE

	No	Yes	Need Help
38. Rarely smiles, giggles, or laughs at funny things	☐	☐	☐
39. Doesn't pay attention to sights and sounds	☐	☐	☐
40. Doesn't seem to watch moving objects	☐	☐	☐
41. Shows no surprise to new events	☐	☐	☐
42. Doesn't react to own name	☐	☐	☐
43. Doesn't care when others are hurt	☐	☐	☐
44. Doesn't play much at all	☐	☐	☐
45. Doesn't enjoy playing with mother or caregiver	☐	☐	☐
46. Isn't upset when toy is taken away	☐	☐	☐
47. Almost never babbles or tries to talk	☐	☐	☐
48. Doesn't react to sounds	☐	☐	☐

Underreactive Raw Score → ☐

DYSREGULATED

	No	Yes	Need Help
49. Often cries too long	☐	☐	☐
50. Often frightened by dreams or the nighttime	☐	☐	☐
51. Screams in sleep and can't be comforted	☐	☐	☐
52. Can't comfort self when upset	☐	☐	☐
53. Wakes up often and doesn't fall back asleep	☐	☐	☐
54. Doesn't have a regular sleep schedule	☐	☐	☐
55. Too often needs help to fall asleep	☐	☐	☐

Dysregulated Raw Score → ☐

III. RESULTS

Add the items marked *Yes* in each of the four subtests, and place the totals in the appropriate boxes marked Raw Score (e.g., *Detached Raw Score*) after each subtest. Transfer those totals to the spaces under the column titled Raw Scores below. Add the four raw scores to calculate the *Temperament & Regulatory Index (TRI),* and place it in the space provided. Determine percentiles and standard scores (or T-scores) of each of these raw scores by using the Conversion Table in the appendix in the **TABS Manual**. (Refer to Chapter 3 of the manual for a discussion of score conversions.) Although not intended for routine assessment purposes, subtest scores might be useful for research or highly specialized clinical purposes. If using subtest scores, carefully review Chapter 4 for information about subtest reliability and the reliability of differences between subtests. If the child's *TRI* indicates that he or she may be at risk for atypical development, early intervention and/or further assessment may be necessary.

	Raw Scores	Percentiles	Standard Scores (or T-scores)
Detached	....	....	....
Hyper-sensitive/active	....	....	....
Underreactive	....	....	....
Dysregulated	....	....	....
Temperament & Regulatory Index (TRI) (total of four factor raw scores)	________	________	________

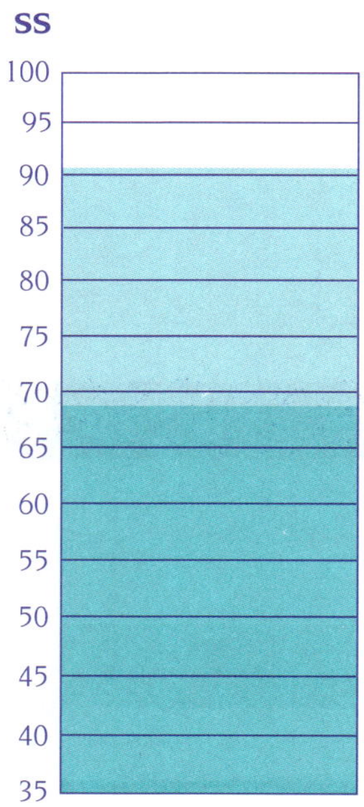

NOTES:

SS = Standard Score (M =100, SD =15)

Typical At-Risk Atypical

 ISBN-13: 978-1-55766-424-2 ISBN-10: 1-55766-424-2
Manufactured in the United States of America.

TABS Assessment Tool

Temperament and Atypical Behavior Scale

Early Childhood Indicators of Developmental Dysfunction

Stephen J. Bagnato, Ed.D., N.C.S.P.
John T. Neisworth, Ph.D.
John Salvia, D.Ed.
Frances M. Hunt, Ph.D.

Instructions for administering the TABS Assessment Tool:

Please refer to Chapter 3 of the **TABS Manual** for important information before administering the TABS Assessment Tool. Complete (or have rater complete) the information in Section I. Read and discuss directions for Section II with the rater, making sure that he or she understands how to respond to the items. Ask the rater to return the Assessment Tool for scoring and interpretation when he or she has completed Section II.

I. CHILD INFORMATION

Name of child: ______________________ Sex: Female ❑ Male ❑

Date of birth: ______________________ Age (in years and months): ______________

Child's address: ______________________

Name of parent or primary caregiver in household: ______________________

Relationship to child: Mother ❑ Father ❑ Other ______________________

Telephone number: ______________________ Best time to contact: ______________

List any previously identified problems or diagnoses for this child.

1. ______________________
2. ______________________
3. ______________________

II. TABS INDICATORS

The following 55 items list some of the most frequent problems in temperament and self-regulation that parents and professionals observe in young children. Read each numbered item and check *No* if the behavior is not a problem. Check *Yes* if the behavior is a problem. For those items marked *Yes*, check *Need Help* if there is special concern and assistance is needed to cope with the behavior. Return this form to the individual administering this Assessment Tool for scoring and interpretation.

Name of rater: ______________________ Date Assessment Tool completed: ______________

Relationship to child: ______________________

DETACHED	No	Yes	Need Help
1. Consistently upset by changes in schedule	☐	☐	☐
2. Emotions don't match what is going on	☐	☐	☐
3. Seems to look through or past people	☐	☐	☐
4. Resists looking you in the eye	☐	☐	☐
5. Acts like others are not there	☐	☐	☐
6. Hardly ever starts on own to play with others	☐	☐	☐
7. Moods and wants are too hard to figure out	☐	☐	☐
8. Seems to be in "own world"	☐	☐	☐
9. Often stares into space	☐	☐	☐
10. "Tunes out," loses contact with what is going on	☐	☐	☐
11. Plays with toys in strange ways	☐	☐	☐
12. Plays with toys as if confused by how they work	☐	☐	☐
13. Makes strange throat noises	☐	☐	☐
14. Disturbed by too much light, noise, or touching	☐	☐	☐
15. Overexcited in crowded places	☐	☐	☐
16. Stares at lights	☐	☐	☐
17. Overly interested in toy/object	☐	☐	☐
18. Flaps hands over and over	☐	☐	☐
19. Shakes head over and over	☐	☐	☐
20. Wanders around without purpose	☐	☐	☐
Detached Raw Score →		☐	

HYPER-SENSITIVE/ACTIVE	No	Yes	Need Help
21. Upset by every little thing	☐	☐	☐
22. Often difficult to soothe when upset and crying	☐	☐	☐
23. Has wide swings in mood	☐	☐	☐
24. Gets angry too easily	☐	☐	☐
25. Too easily frustrated	☐	☐	☐
26. Has wild temper tantrums	☐	☐	☐
27. Frequently irritable, "touchy," or fussy	☐	☐	☐
28. Can't wait at all for food or toy	☐	☐	☐
29. Demands attention continually	☐	☐	☐
30. Controls adult's behavior, "is the boss"	☐	☐	☐

	No	Yes	Need Help
31. Jealous too often	☐	☐	☐
32. Mostly on the go, "in high gear"	☐	☐	☐
33. Doesn't sit still	☐	☐	☐
34. Too "grabby," impulsive	☐	☐	☐
35. Almost always refuses to do what is told	☐	☐	☐
36. Throws or breaks things on purpose	☐	☐	☐
37. Bites, hits, kicks others	☐	☐	☐

Hyper-sensitive/active Raw Score → ☐

UNDERREACTIVE

	No	Yes	Need Help
38. Rarely smiles, giggles, or laughs at funny things	☐	☐	☐
39. Doesn't pay attention to sights and sounds	☐	☐	☐
40. Doesn't seem to watch moving objects	☐	☐	☐
41. Shows no surprise to new events	☐	☐	☐
42. Doesn't react to own name	☐	☐	☐
43. Doesn't care when others are hurt	☐	☐	☐
44. Doesn't play much at all	☐	☐	☐
45. Doesn't enjoy playing with mother or caregiver	☐	☐	☐
46. Isn't upset when toy is taken away	☐	☐	☐
47. Almost never babbles or tries to talk	☐	☐	☐
48. Doesn't react to sounds	☐	☐	☐

Underreactive Raw Score → ☐

DYSREGULATED

	No	Yes	Need Help
49. Often cries too long	☐	☐	☐
50. Often frightened by dreams or the nighttime	☐	☐	☐
51. Screams in sleep and can't be comforted	☐	☐	☐
52. Can't comfort self when upset	☐	☐	☐
53. Wakes up often and doesn't fall back asleep	☐	☐	☐
54. Doesn't have a regular sleep schedule	☐	☐	☐
55. Too often needs help to fall asleep	☐	☐	☐

Dysregulated Raw Score → ☐

III. RESULTS

Add the items marked *Yes* in each of the four subtests, and place the totals in the appropriate boxes marked Raw Score (e.g., *Detached Raw Score*) after each subtest. Transfer those totals to the spaces under the column titled Raw Scores below. Add the four raw scores to calculate the *Temperament & Regulatory Index (TRI)*, and place it in the space provided. Determine percentiles and standard scores (or T-scores) of each of these raw scores by using the Conversion Table in the appendix in the **TABS Manual**. (Refer to Chapter 3 of the manual for a discussion of score conversions.) Although not intended for routine assessment purposes, subtest scores might be useful for research or highly specialized clinical purposes. If using subtest scores, carefully review Chapter 4 for information about subtest reliability and the reliability of differences between subtests. If the child's *TRI* indicates that he or she may be at risk for atypical development, early intervention and/or further assessment may be necessary.

	Raw Scores	Percentiles	Standard Scores (or T-scores)
Detached	....	....	....
Hyper-sensitive/active	....	....	....
Underreactive	....	....	....
Dysregulated	....	....	....
Temperament & Regulatory Index (TRI) (total of four factor raw scores)	________	________	________

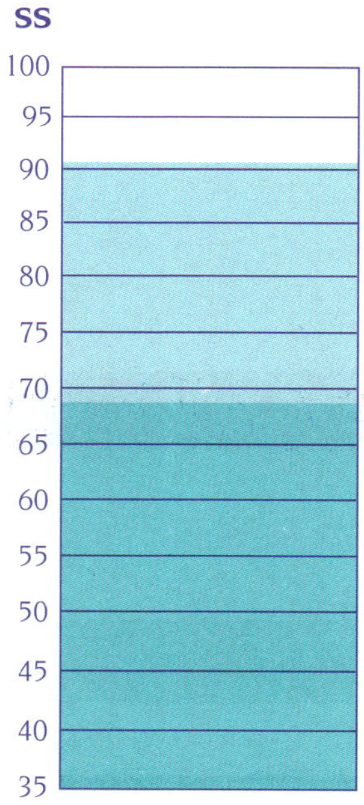

NOTES:

SS = Standard Score (M =100, SD =15)

☐ Typical ☐ At-Risk ☐ Atypical

 ISBN-13: 978-1-55766-424-2 ISBN-10: 1-55766-424-2
Manufactured in the United States of America.

TABS Assessment Tool

Temperament and Atypical Behavior Scale

Early Childhood Indicators of Developmental Dysfunction

Stephen J. Bagnato, Ed.D., N.C.S.P. | John T. Neisworth, Ph.D.
John Salvia, D.Ed. | Frances M. Hunt, Ph.D.

Instructions for administering the TABS Assessment Tool:

Please refer to Chapter 3 of the **TABS Manual** for important information before administering the TABS Assessment Tool. Complete (or have rater complete) the information in Section I. Read and discuss directions for Section II with the rater, making sure that he or she understands how to respond to the items. Ask the rater to return the Assessment Tool for scoring and interpretation when he or she has completed Section II.

I. CHILD INFORMATION

Name of child: ______________________ Sex: Female ❑ Male ❑

Date of birth: ______________________ Age (in years and months): ______________

Child's address: ____

Name of parent or primary caregiver in household: ______________________

Relationship to child: Mother ❑ Father ❑ Other ______________________

Telephone number: ______________________ Best time to contact: ______________

List any previously identified problems or diagnoses for this child.

1. ____
2. ____
3. ____

II. TABS INDICATORS

The following 55 items list some of the most frequent problems in temperament and self-regulation that parents and professionals observe in young children. Read each numbered item and check *No* if the behavior is not a problem. Check *Yes* if the behavior is a problem. For those items marked *Yes*, check *Need Help* if there is special concern and assistance is needed to cope with the behavior. Return this form to the individual administering this Assessment Tool for scoring and interpretation.

Name of rater: ______________________ Date Assessment Tool completed: ______________

Relationship to child: ____

DETACHED	No	Yes	Need Help
1. Consistently upset by changes in schedule	☐	☐	☐
2. Emotions don't match what is going on	☐	☐	☐
3. Seems to look through or past people	☐	☐	☐
4. Resists looking you in the eye	☐	☐	☐
5. Acts like others are not there	☐	☐	☐
6. Hardly ever starts on own to play with others	☐	☐	☐
7. Moods and wants are too hard to figure out	☐	☐	☐
8. Seems to be in "own world"	☐	☐	☐
9. Often stares into space	☐	☐	☐
10. "Tunes out," loses contact with what is going on	☐	☐	☐
11. Plays with toys in strange ways	☐	☐	☐
12. Plays with toys as if confused by how they work	☐	☐	☐
13. Makes strange throat noises	☐	☐	☐
14. Disturbed by too much light, noise, or touching	☐	☐	☐
15. Overexcited in crowded places	☐	☐	☐
16. Stares at lights	☐	☐	☐
17. Overly interested in toy/object	☐	☐	☐
18. Flaps hands over and over	☐	☐	☐
19. Shakes head over and over	☐	☐	☐
20. Wanders around without purpose	☐	☐	☐
Detached Raw Score →		☐	

HYPER-SENSITIVE/ACTIVE	No	Yes	Need Help
21. Upset by every little thing	☐	☐	☐
22. Often difficult to soothe when upset and crying	☐	☐	☐
23. Has wide swings in mood	☐	☐	☐
24. Gets angry too easily	☐	☐	☐
25. Too easily frustrated	☐	☐	☐
26. Has wild temper tantrums	☐	☐	☐
27. Frequently irritable, "touchy," or fussy	☐	☐	☐
28. Can't wait at all for food or toy	☐	☐	☐
29. Demands attention continually	☐	☐	☐
30. Controls adult's behavior, "is the boss"	☐	☐	☐

	No	Yes	Need Help
31. Jealous too often	☐	☐	☐
32. Mostly on the go, "in high gear"	☐	☐	☐
33. Doesn't sit still	☐	☐	☐
34. Too "grabby," impulsive	☐	☐	☐
35. Almost always refuses to do what is told	☐	☐	☐
36. Throws or breaks things on purpose	☐	☐	☐
37. Bites, hits, kicks others	☐	☐	☐

Hyper-sensitive/active Raw Score → ☐

UNDERREACTIVE

	No	Yes	Need Help
38. Rarely smiles, giggles, or laughs at funny things	☐	☐	☐
39. Doesn't pay attention to sights and sounds	☐	☐	☐
40. Doesn't seem to watch moving objects	☐	☐	☐
41. Shows no surprise to new events	☐	☐	☐
42. Doesn't react to own name	☐	☐	☐
43. Doesn't care when others are hurt	☐	☐	☐
44. Doesn't play much at all	☐	☐	☐
45. Doesn't enjoy playing with mother or caregiver	☐	☐	☐
46. Isn't upset when toy is taken away	☐	☐	☐
47. Almost never babbles or tries to talk	☐	☐	☐
48. Doesn't react to sounds	☐	☐	☐

Underreactive Raw Score → ☐

DYSREGULATED

	No	Yes	Need Help
49. Often cries too long	☐	☐	☐
50. Often frightened by dreams or the nighttime	☐	☐	☐
51. Screams in sleep and can't be comforted	☐	☐	☐
52. Can't comfort self when upset	☐	☐	☐
53. Wakes up often and doesn't fall back asleep	☐	☐	☐
54. Doesn't have a regular sleep schedule	☐	☐	☐
55. Too often needs help to fall asleep	☐	☐	☐

Dysregulated Raw Score → ☐

III. RESULTS

Add the items marked *Yes* in each of the four subtests, and place the totals in the appropriate boxes marked Raw Score (e.g., *Detached Raw Score*) after each subtest. Transfer those totals to the spaces under the column titled Raw Scores below. Add the four raw scores to calculate the *Temperament & Regulatory Index (TRI)*, and place it in the space provided. Determine percentiles and standard scores (or T-scores) of each of these raw scores by using the Conversion Table in the appendix in the **TABS Manual**. (Refer to Chapter 3 of the manual for a discussion of score conversions.) Although not intended for routine assessment purposes, subtest scores might be useful for research or highly specialized clinical purposes. If using subtest scores, carefully review Chapter 4 for information about subtest reliability and the reliability of differences between subtests. If the child's *TRI* indicates that he or she may be at risk for atypical development, early intervention and/or further assessment may be necessary.

	Raw Scores	Percentiles	Standard Scores (or T-scores)
Detached	....	....	....
Hyper-sensitive/active	....	....	....
Underreactive	....	....	....
Dysregulated	....	....	....
Temperament & Regulatory Index (TRI) (total of four factor raw scores)	________	________	________

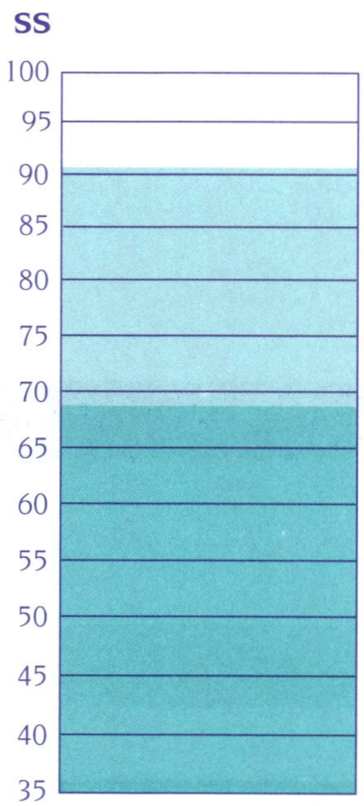

NOTES:

SS = Standard Score (*M* =100, *SD* =15)

☐ Typical ☐ At-Risk ☐ Atypical

 ISBN-13: 978-1-55766-424-2 ISBN-10: 1-55766-424-2
Manufactured in the United States of America.

TABS Assessment Tool

Temperament and Atypical Behavior Scale

Early Childhood Indicators of Developmental Dysfunction

Stephen J. Bagnato, Ed.D., N.C.S.P.
John T. Neisworth, Ph.D.
John Salvia, D.Ed.
Frances M. Hunt, Ph.D.

Instructions for administering the TABS Assessment Tool:

Please refer to Chapter 3 of the **TABS Manual** for important information before administering the TABS Assessment Tool. Complete (or have rater complete) the information in Section I. Read and discuss directions for Section II with the rater, making sure that he or she understands how to respond to the items. Ask the rater to return the Assessment Tool for scoring and interpretation when he or she has completed Section II.

I. CHILD INFORMATION

Name of child: ______________________________ Sex: Female ❑ Male ❑

Date of birth: ______________________ Age (in years and months): ______________

Child's address: ____

Name of parent or primary caregiver in household: ______________________________

Relationship to child: Mother ❑ Father ❑ Other ______________________

Telephone number: ______________________ Best time to contact: ______________

List any previously identified problems or diagnoses for this child.

1. ____
2. ____
3. ____

II. TABS INDICATORS

The following 55 items list some of the most frequent problems in temperament and self-regulation that parents and professionals observe in young children. Read each numbered item and check *No* if the behavior is not a problem. Check *Yes* if the behavior is a problem. For those items marked *Yes*, check *Need Help* if there is special concern and assistance is needed to cope with the behavior. Return this form to the individual administering this Assessment Tool for scoring and interpretation.

Name of rater: ______________________ Date Assessment Tool completed: ______________

Relationship to child: ____

1-800-638-3775 www.brookespublishing.com

DETACHED	No	Yes	Need Help
1. Consistently upset by changes in schedule	☐	☐	☐
2. Emotions don't match what is going on	☐	☐	☐
3. Seems to look through or past people	☐	☐	☐
4. Resists looking you in the eye	☐	☐	☐
5. Acts like others are not there	☐	☐	☐
6. Hardly ever starts on own to play with others	☐	☐	☐
7. Moods and wants are too hard to figure out	☐	☐	☐
8. Seems to be in "own world"	☐	☐	☐
9. Often stares into space	☐	☐	☐
10. "Tunes out," loses contact with what is going on	☐	☐	☐
11. Plays with toys in strange ways	☐	☐	☐
12. Plays with toys as if confused by how they work	☐	☐	☐
13. Makes strange throat noises	☐	☐	☐
14. Disturbed by too much light, noise, or touching	☐	☐	☐
15. Overexcited in crowded places	☐	☐	☐
16. Stares at lights	☐	☐	☐
17. Overly interested in toy/object	☐	☐	☐
18. Flaps hands over and over	☐	☐	☐
19. Shakes head over and over	☐	☐	☐
20. Wanders around without purpose	☐	☐	☐
Detached Raw Score →		☐	

HYPER-SENSITIVE/ACTIVE	No	Yes	Need Help
21. Upset by every little thing	☐	☐	☐
22. Often difficult to soothe when upset and crying	☐	☐	☐
23. Has wide swings in mood	☐	☐	☐
24. Gets angry too easily	☐	☐	☐
25. Too easily frustrated	☐	☐	☐
26. Has wild temper tantrums	☐	☐	☐
27. Frequently irritable, "touchy," or fussy	☐	☐	☐
28. Can't wait at all for food or toy	☐	☐	☐
29. Demands attention continually	☐	☐	☐
30. Controls adult's behavior, "is the boss"	☐	☐	☐

	No	Yes	Need Help
31. Jealous too often	☐	☐	☐
32. Mostly on the go, "in high gear"	☐	☐	☐
33. Doesn't sit still	☐	☐	☐
34. Too "grabby," impulsive	☐	☐	☐
35. Almost always refuses to do what is told	☐	☐	☐
36. Throws or breaks things on purpose	☐	☐	☐
37. Bites, hits, kicks others	☐	☐	☐

Hyper-sensitive/active Raw Score → ☐

UNDERREACTIVE

	No	Yes	Need Help
38. Rarely smiles, giggles, or laughs at funny things	☐	☐	☐
39. Doesn't pay attention to sights and sounds	☐	☐	☐
40. Doesn't seem to watch moving objects	☐	☐	☐
41. Shows no surprise to new events	☐	☐	☐
42. Doesn't react to own name	☐	☐	☐
43. Doesn't care when others are hurt	☐	☐	☐
44. Doesn't play much at all	☐	☐	☐
45. Doesn't enjoy playing with mother or caregiver	☐	☐	☐
46. Isn't upset when toy is taken away	☐	☐	☐
47. Almost never babbles or tries to talk	☐	☐	☐
48. Doesn't react to sounds	☐	☐	☐

Underreactive Raw Score → ☐

DYSREGULATED

	No	Yes	Need Help
49. Often cries too long	☐	☐	☐
50. Often frightened by dreams or the nighttime	☐	☐	☐
51. Screams in sleep and can't be comforted	☐	☐	☐
52. Can't comfort self when upset	☐	☐	☐
53. Wakes up often and doesn't fall back asleep	☐	☐	☐
54. Doesn't have a regular sleep schedule	☐	☐	☐
55. Too often needs help to fall asleep	☐	☐	☐

Dysregulated Raw Score → ☐

III. RESULTS

Add the items marked *Yes* in each of the four subtests, and place the totals in the appropriate boxes marked Raw Score (e.g., *Detached Raw Score*) after each subtest. Transfer those totals to the spaces under the column titled Raw Scores below. Add the four raw scores to calculate the *Temperament & Regulatory Index (TRI),* and place it in the space provided. Determine percentiles and standard scores (or T-scores) of each of these raw scores by using the Conversion Table in the appendix in the **TABS Manual**. (Refer to Chapter 3 of the manual for a discussion of score conversions.) Although not intended for routine assessment purposes, subtest scores might be useful for research or highly specialized clinical purposes. If using subtest scores, carefully review Chapter 4 for information about subtest reliability and the reliability of differences between subtests. If the child's *TRI* indicates that he or she may be at risk for atypical development, early intervention and/or further assessment may be necessary.

	Raw Scores	Percentiles	Standard Scores (or T-scores)
Detached			
Hyper-sensitive/active			
Underreactive			
Dysregulated			
Temperament & Regulatory Index (TRI) (total of four factor raw scores)			

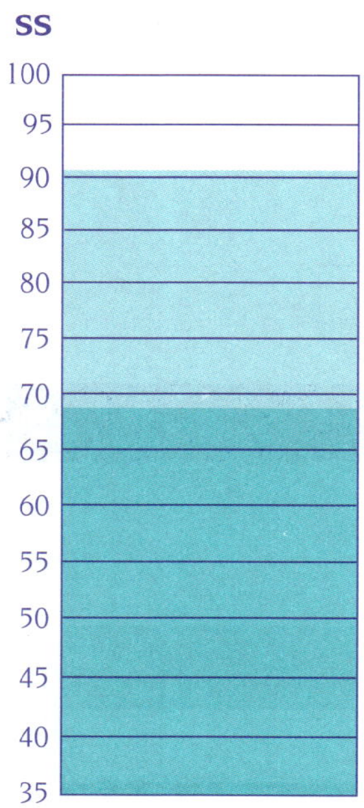

SS = Standard Score (*M* =100, *SD* =15)

☐ Typical ☐ At-Risk ☐ Atypical

NOTES:

 ISBN-13: 978-1-55766-424-2 ISBN-10: 1-55766-424-2
Manufactured in the United States of America.

TABS Assessment Tool

Temperament and Atypical Behavior Scale

Early Childhood Indicators of Developmental Dysfunction

Stephen J. Bagnato, Ed.D., N.C.S.P. | John T. Neisworth, Ph.D.
John Salvia, D.Ed. | Frances M. Hunt, Ph.D.

Instructions for administering the TABS Assessment Tool:

Please refer to Chapter 3 of the **TABS Manual** for important information before administering the TABS Assessment Tool. Complete (or have rater complete) the information in Section I. Read and discuss directions for Section II with the rater, making sure that he or she understands how to respond to the items. Ask the rater to return the Assessment Tool for scoring and interpretation when he or she has completed Section II.

I. CHILD INFORMATION

Name of child: ______________________ Sex: Female ❑ Male ❑

Date of birth: ______________________ Age (in years and months): ______________________

Child's address: ______________________

Name of parent or primary caregiver in household: ______________________

Relationship to child: Mother ❑ Father ❑ Other ______________________

Telephone number: ______________________ Best time to contact: ______________________

List any previously identified problems or diagnoses for this child.

1. ______________________
2. ______________________
3. ______________________

II. TABS INDICATORS

The following 55 items list some of the most frequent problems in temperament and self-regulation that parents and professionals observe in young children. Read each numbered item and check *No* if the behavior is not a problem. Check *Yes* if the behavior is a problem. For those items marked *Yes*, check *Need Help* if there is special concern and assistance is needed to cope with the behavior. Return this form to the individual administering this Assessment Tool for scoring and interpretation.

Name of rater: ______________________ Date Assessment Tool completed: ______________________

Relationship to child: ______________________

DETACHED	No	Yes	Need Help
1. Consistently upset by changes in schedule	☐	☐	☐
2. Emotions don't match what is going on	☐	☐	☐
3. Seems to look through or past people	☐	☐	☐
4. Resists looking you in the eye	☐	☐	☐
5. Acts like others are not there	☐	☐	☐
6. Hardly ever starts on own to play with others	☐	☐	☐
7. Moods and wants are too hard to figure out	☐	☐	☐
8. Seems to be in "own world"	☐	☐	☐
9. Often stares into space	☐	☐	☐
10. "Tunes out," loses contact with what is going on	☐	☐	☐
11. Plays with toys in strange ways	☐	☐	☐
12. Plays with toys as if confused by how they work	☐	☐	☐
13. Makes strange throat noises	☐	☐	☐
14. Disturbed by too much light, noise, or touching	☐	☐	☐
15. Overexcited in crowded places	☐	☐	☐
16. Stares at lights	☐	☐	☐
17. Overly interested in toy/object	☐	☐	☐
18. Flaps hands over and over	☐	☐	☐
19. Shakes head over and over	☐	☐	☐
20. Wanders around without purpose	☐	☐	☐
Detached Raw Score →		☐	

HYPER-SENSITIVE/ACTIVE	No	Yes	Need Help
21. Upset by every little thing	☐	☐	☐
22. Often difficult to soothe when upset and crying	☐	☐	☐
23. Has wide swings in mood	☐	☐	☐
24. Gets angry too easily	☐	☐	☐
25. Too easily frustrated	☐	☐	☐
26. Has wild temper tantrums	☐	☐	☐
27. Frequently irritable, "touchy," or fussy	☐	☐	☐
28. Can't wait at all for food or toy	☐	☐	☐
29. Demands attention continually	☐	☐	☐
30. Controls adult's behavior, "is the boss"	☐	☐	☐

	No	Yes	Need Help
31. Jealous too often	☐	☐	☐
32. Mostly on the go, "in high gear"	☐	☐	☐
33. Doesn't sit still	☐	☐	☐
34. Too "grabby," impulsive	☐	☐	☐
35. Almost always refuses to do what is told	☐	☐	☐
36. Throws or breaks things on purpose	☐	☐	☐
37. Bites, hits, kicks others	☐	☐	☐

Hyper-sensitive/active Raw Score → ☐

UNDERREACTIVE

	No	Yes	Need Help
38. Rarely smiles, giggles, or laughs at funny things	☐	☐	☐
39. Doesn't pay attention to sights and sounds	☐	☐	☐
40. Doesn't seem to watch moving objects	☐	☐	☐
41. Shows no surprise to new events	☐	☐	☐
42. Doesn't react to own name	☐	☐	☐
43. Doesn't care when others are hurt	☐	☐	☐
44. Doesn't play much at all	☐	☐	☐
45. Doesn't enjoy playing with mother or caregiver	☐	☐	☐
46. Isn't upset when toy is taken away	☐	☐	☐
47. Almost never babbles or tries to talk	☐	☐	☐
48. Doesn't react to sounds	☐	☐	☐

Underreactive Raw Score → ☐

DYSREGULATED

	No	Yes	Need Help
49. Often cries too long	☐	☐	☐
50. Often frightened by dreams or the nighttime	☐	☐	☐
51. Screams in sleep and can't be comforted	☐	☐	☐
52. Can't comfort self when upset	☐	☐	☐
53. Wakes up often and doesn't fall back asleep	☐	☐	☐
54. Doesn't have a regular sleep schedule	☐	☐	☐
55. Too often needs help to fall asleep	☐	☐	☐

Dysregulated Raw Score → ☐

III. RESULTS

Add the items marked *Yes* in each of the four subtests, and place the totals in the appropriate boxes marked Raw Score (e.g., *Detached Raw Score*) after each subtest. Transfer those totals to the spaces under the column titled Raw Scores below. Add the four raw scores to calculate the *Temperament & Regulatory Index (TRI)*, and place it in the space provided. Determine percentiles and standard scores (or T-scores) of each of these raw scores by using the Conversion Table in the appendix in the **TABS Manual**. (Refer to Chapter 3 of the manual for a discussion of score conversions.) Although not intended for routine assessment purposes, subtest scores might be useful for research or highly specialized clinical purposes. If using subtest scores, carefully review Chapter 4 for information about subtest reliability and the reliability of differences between subtests. If the child's *TRI* indicates that he or she may be at risk for atypical development, early intervention and/or further assessment may be necessary.

	Raw Scores	Percentiles	Standard Scores (or T-scores)
Detached	....	....	....
Hyper-sensitive/active	....	....	....
Underreactive	....	....	....
Dysregulated	....	....	....
Temperament & Regulatory Index (TRI) (total of four factor raw scores)	________	________	________

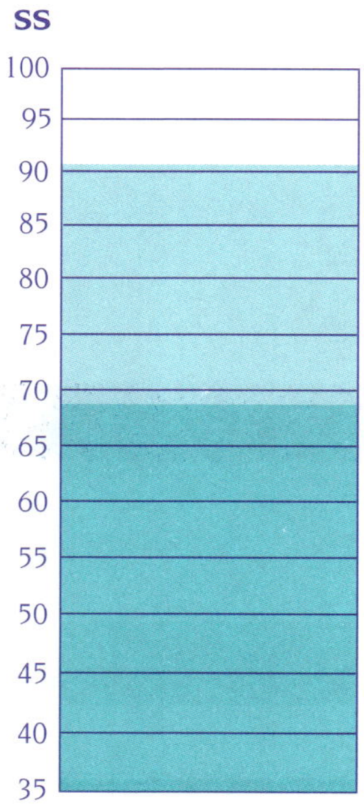

NOTES:

SS = Standard Score (*M* =100, *SD* =15)

☐ Typical ☐ At-Risk ☐ Atypical

 ISBN-13: 978-1-55766-424-2 ISBN-10: 1-55766-424-2
Manufactured in the United States of America.

TABS Assessment Tool

Temperament and Atypical Behavior Scale

Early Childhood Indicators of Developmental Dysfunction

Stephen J. Bagnato, Ed.D., N.C.S.P. | John T. Neisworth, Ph.D.
John Salvia, D.Ed. | Frances M. Hunt, Ph.D.

Instructions for administering the TABS Assessment Tool:

Please refer to Chapter 3 of the **TABS Manual** for important information before administering the TABS Assessment Tool. Complete (or have rater complete) the information in Section I. Read and discuss directions for Section II with the rater, making sure that he or she understands how to respond to the items. Ask the rater to return the Assessment Tool for scoring and interpretation when he or she has completed Section II.

I. CHILD INFORMATION

Name of child: ______________________ Sex: Female ❑ Male ❑

Date of birth: ______________________ Age (in years and months): ______________________

Child's address: ______________________

Name of parent or primary caregiver in household: ______________________

Relationship to child: Mother ❑ Father ❑ Other ______________________

Telephone number: ______________________ Best time to contact: ______________________

List any previously identified problems or diagnoses for this child.

1. ______________________
2. ______________________
3. ______________________

II. TABS INDICATORS

The following 55 items list some of the most frequent problems in temperament and self-regulation that parents and professionals observe in young children. Read each numbered item and check *No* if the behavior is not a problem. Check *Yes* if the behavior is a problem. For those items marked *Yes*, check *Need Help* if there is special concern and assistance is needed to cope with the behavior. Return this form to the individual administering this Assessment Tool for scoring and interpretation.

Name of rater: ______________________ Date Assessment Tool completed: ______________________

Relationship to child: ______________________

DETACHED	No	Yes	Need Help
1. Consistently upset by changes in schedule	☐	☐	☐
2. Emotions don't match what is going on	☐	☐	☐
3. Seems to look through or past people	☐	☐	☐
4. Resists looking you in the eye	☐	☐	☐
5. Acts like others are not there	☐	☐	☐
6. Hardly ever starts on own to play with others	☐	☐	☐
7. Moods and wants are too hard to figure out	☐	☐	☐
8. Seems to be in "own world"	☐	☐	☐
9. Often stares into space	☐	☐	☐
10. "Tunes out," loses contact with what is going on	☐	☐	☐
11. Plays with toys in strange ways	☐	☐	☐
12. Plays with toys as if confused by how they work	☐	☐	☐
13. Makes strange throat noises	☐	☐	☐
14. Disturbed by too much light, noise, or touching	☐	☐	☐
15. Overexcited in crowded places	☐	☐	☐
16. Stares at lights	☐	☐	☐
17. Overly interested in toy/object	☐	☐	☐
18. Flaps hands over and over	☐	☐	☐
19. Shakes head over and over	☐	☐	☐
20. Wanders around without purpose	☐	☐	☐
Detached Raw Score →		☐	

HYPER-SENSITIVE/ACTIVE	No	Yes	Need Help
21. Upset by every little thing	☐	☐	☐
22. Often difficult to soothe when upset and crying	☐	☐	☐
23. Has wide swings in mood	☐	☐	☐
24. Gets angry too easily	☐	☐	☐
25. Too easily frustrated	☐	☐	☐
26. Has wild temper tantrums	☐	☐	☐
27. Frequently irritable, "touchy," or fussy	☐	☐	☐
28. Can't wait at all for food or toy	☐	☐	☐
29. Demands attention continually	☐	☐	☐
30. Controls adult's behavior, "is the boss"	☐	☐	☐

	No	Yes	Need Help
31. Jealous too often	☐	☐	☐
32. Mostly on the go, "in high gear"	☐	☐	☐
33. Doesn't sit still	☐	☐	☐
34. Too "grabby," impulsive	☐	☐	☐
35. Almost always refuses to do what is told	☐	☐	☐
36. Throws or breaks things on purpose	☐	☐	☐
37. Bites, hits, kicks others	☐	☐	☐
Hyper-sensitive/active Raw Score →		☐	

UNDERREACTIVE

	No	Yes	Need Help
38. Rarely smiles, giggles, or laughs at funny things	☐	☐	☐
39. Doesn't pay attention to sights and sounds	☐	☐	☐
40. Doesn't seem to watch moving objects	☐	☐	☐
41. Shows no surprise to new events	☐	☐	☐
42. Doesn't react to own name	☐	☐	☐
43. Doesn't care when others are hurt	☐	☐	☐
44. Doesn't play much at all	☐	☐	☐
45. Doesn't enjoy playing with mother or caregiver	☐	☐	☐
46. Isn't upset when toy is taken away	☐	☐	☐
47. Almost never babbles or tries to talk	☐	☐	☐
48. Doesn't react to sounds	☐	☐	☐
Underreactive Raw Score →		☐	

DYSREGULATED

	No	Yes	Need Help
49. Often cries too long	☐	☐	☐
50. Often frightened by dreams or the nighttime	☐	☐	☐
51. Screams in sleep and can't be comforted	☐	☐	☐
52. Can't comfort self when upset	☐	☐	☐
53. Wakes up often and doesn't fall back asleep	☐	☐	☐
54. Doesn't have a regular sleep schedule	☐	☐	☐
55. Too often needs help to fall asleep	☐	☐	☐
Dysregulated Raw Score →		☐	

III. RESULTS

Add the items marked *Yes* in each of the four subtests, and place the totals in the appropriate boxes marked Raw Score (e.g., *Detached Raw Score*) after each subtest. Transfer those totals to the spaces under the column titled Raw Scores below. Add the four raw scores to calculate the *Temperament & Regulatory Index (TRI),* and place it in the space provided. Determine percentiles and standard scores (or T-scores) of each of these raw scores by using the Conversion Table in the appendix in the **TABS Manual**. (Refer to Chapter 3 of the manual for a discussion of score conversions.) Although not intended for routine assessment purposes, subtest scores might be useful for research or highly specialized clinical purposes. If using subtest scores, carefully review Chapter 4 for information about subtest reliability and the reliability of differences between subtests. If the child's *TRI* indicates that he or she may be at risk for atypical development, early intervention and/or further assessment may be necessary.

	Raw Scores	Percentiles	Standard Scores (or T-scores)
Detached	....	....	....
Hyper-sensitive/active	....	....	....
Underreactive	....	....	....
Dysregulated	....	....	....
Temperament & Regulatory Index (TRI) (total of four factor raw scores)	________	________	________

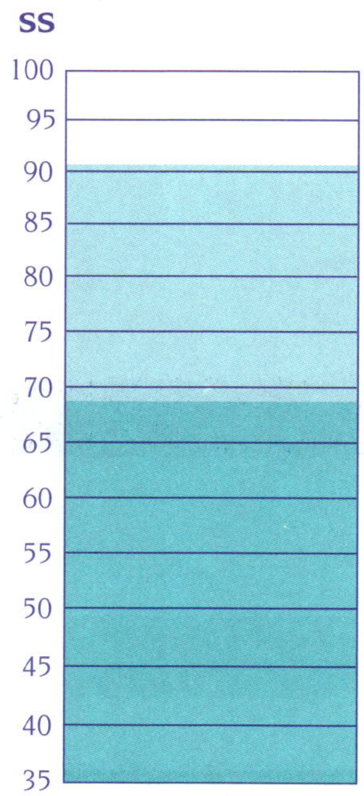

NOTES:

SS = Standard Score (M =100, SD =15)

☐ Typical ☐ At-Risk ☐ Atypical

 ISBN-13: 978-1-55766-424-2 ISBN-10: 1-55766-424-2
Manufactured in the United States of America.

TABS Assessment Tool

Temperament and Atypical Behavior Scale

Early Childhood Indicators of Developmental Dysfunction

Stephen J. Bagnato, Ed.D., N.C.S.P.
John T. Neisworth, Ph.D.
John Salvia, D.Ed.
Frances M. Hunt, Ph.D.

Instructions for administering the TABS Assessment Tool:

Please refer to Chapter 3 of the **TABS Manual** for important information before administering the TABS Assessment Tool. Complete (or have rater complete) the information in Section I. Read and discuss directions for Section II with the rater, making sure that he or she understands how to respond to the items. Ask the rater to return the Assessment Tool for scoring and interpretation when he or she has completed Section II.

I. CHILD INFORMATION

Name of child: ______________________ Sex: Female ❑ Male ❑

Date of birth: ______________________ Age (in years and months): ______________________

Child's address: ______________________

Name of parent or primary caregiver in household: ______________________

Relationship to child: Mother ❑ Father ❑ Other ______________________

Telephone number: ______________________ Best time to contact: ______________________

List any previously identified problems or diagnoses for this child.

1. ______________________
2. ______________________
3. ______________________

II. TABS INDICATORS

The following 55 items list some of the most frequent problems in temperament and self-regulation that parents and professionals observe in young children. Read each numbered item and check *No* if the behavior is not a problem. Check *Yes* if the behavior is a problem. For those items marked *Yes*, check *Need Help* if there is special concern and assistance is needed to cope with the behavior. Return this form to the individual administering this Assessment Tool for scoring and interpretation.

Name of rater: ______________________ Date Assessment Tool completed: ______________________

Relationship to child: ______________________

1-800-638-3775 www.brookespublishing.com

DETACHED	No	Yes	Need Help
1. Consistently upset by changes in schedule	☐	☐	☐
2. Emotions don't match what is going on	☐	☐	☐
3. Seems to look through or past people	☐	☐	☐
4. Resists looking you in the eye	☐	☐	☐
5. Acts like others are not there	☐	☐	☐
6. Hardly ever starts on own to play with others	☐	☐	☐
7. Moods and wants are too hard to figure out	☐	☐	☐
8. Seems to be in "own world"	☐	☐	☐
9. Often stares into space	☐	☐	☐
10. "Tunes out," loses contact with what is going on	☐	☐	☐
11. Plays with toys in strange ways	☐	☐	☐
12. Plays with toys as if confused by how they work	☐	☐	☐
13. Makes strange throat noises	☐	☐	☐
14. Disturbed by too much light, noise, or touching	☐	☐	☐
15. Overexcited in crowded places	☐	☐	☐
16. Stares at lights	☐	☐	☐
17. Overly interested in toy/object	☐	☐	☐
18. Flaps hands over and over	☐	☐	☐
19. Shakes head over and over	☐	☐	☐
20. Wanders around without purpose	☐	☐	☐
Detached Raw Score →		☐	

HYPER-SENSITIVE/ACTIVE	No	Yes	Need Help
21. Upset by every little thing	☐	☐	☐
22. Often difficult to soothe when upset and crying	☐	☐	☐
23. Has wide swings in mood	☐	☐	☐
24. Gets angry too easily	☐	☐	☐
25. Too easily frustrated	☐	☐	☐
26. Has wild temper tantrums	☐	☐	☐
27. Frequently irritable, "touchy," or fussy	☐	☐	☐
28. Can't wait at all for food or toy	☐	☐	☐
29. Demands attention continually	☐	☐	☐
30. Controls adult's behavior, "is the boss"	☐	☐	☐

	No	Yes	Need Help
31. Jealous too often	☐	☐	☐
32. Mostly on the go, "in high gear"	☐	☐	☐
33. Doesn't sit still	☐	☐	☐
34. Too "grabby," impulsive	☐	☐	☐
35. Almost always refuses to do what is told	☐	☐	☐
36. Throws or breaks things on purpose	☐	☐	☐
37. Bites, hits, kicks others	☐	☐	☐
Hyper-sensitive/active Raw Score →		☐	

UNDERREACTIVE

	No	Yes	Need Help
38. Rarely smiles, giggles, or laughs at funny things	☐	☐	☐
39. Doesn't pay attention to sights and sounds	☐	☐	☐
40. Doesn't seem to watch moving objects	☐	☐	☐
41. Shows no surprise to new events	☐	☐	☐
42. Doesn't react to own name	☐	☐	☐
43. Doesn't care when others are hurt	☐	☐	☐
44. Doesn't play much at all	☐	☐	☐
45. Doesn't enjoy playing with mother or caregiver	☐	☐	☐
46. Isn't upset when toy is taken away	☐	☐	☐
47. Almost never babbles or tries to talk	☐	☐	☐
48. Doesn't react to sounds	☐	☐	☐
Underreactive Raw Score →		☐	

DYSREGULATED

	No	Yes	Need Help
49. Often cries too long	☐	☐	☐
50. Often frightened by dreams or the nighttime	☐	☐	☐
51. Screams in sleep and can't be comforted	☐	☐	☐
52. Can't comfort self when upset	☐	☐	☐
53. Wakes up often and doesn't fall back asleep	☐	☐	☐
54. Doesn't have a regular sleep schedule	☐	☐	☐
55. Too often needs help to fall asleep	☐	☐	☐
Dysregulated Raw Score →		☐	

III. RESULTS

Add the items marked *Yes* in each of the four subtests, and place the totals in the appropriate boxes marked Raw Score (e.g., *Detached Raw Score*) after each subtest. Transfer those totals to the spaces under the column titled Raw Scores below. Add the four raw scores to calculate the *Temperament & Regulatory Index (TRI)*, and place it in the space provided. Determine percentiles and standard scores (or T-scores) of each of these raw scores by using the Conversion Table in the appendix in the **TABS Manual**. (Refer to Chapter 3 of the manual for a discussion of score conversions.) Although not intended for routine assessment purposes, subtest scores might be useful for research or highly specialized clinical purposes. If using subtest scores, carefully review Chapter 4 for information about subtest reliability and the reliability of differences between subtests. If the child's *TRI* indicates that he or she may be at risk for atypical development, early intervention and/or further assessment may be necessary.

	Raw Scores	Percentiles	Standard Scores (or T-scores)
Detached			
Hyper-sensitive/active			
Underreactive			
Dysregulated			
Temperament & Regulatory Index (TRI) (total of four factor raw scores)			

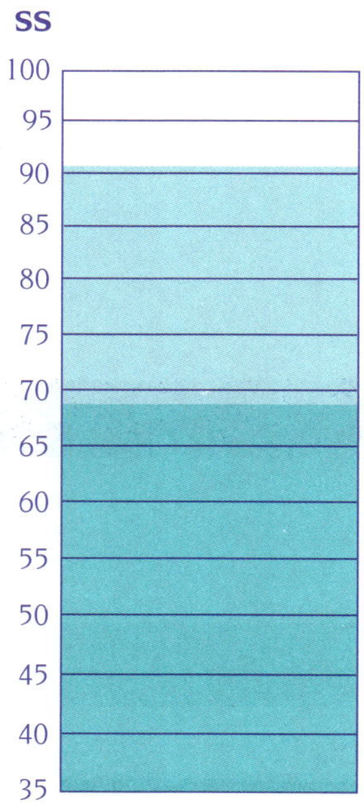

NOTES:

SS = Standard Score (*M* =100, *SD* =15)

☐ Typical ☐ At-Risk ☐ Atypical

 ISBN-13: 978-1-55766-424-2 ISBN-10: 1-55766-424-2
Manufactured in the United States of America.

TABS Assessment Tool

Temperament and Atypical Behavior Scale

Early Childhood Indicators of Developmental Dysfunction

Stephen J. Bagnato, Ed.D., N.C.S.P. John T. Neisworth, Ph.D.

John Salvia, D.Ed. Frances M. Hunt, Ph.D.

Instructions for administering the TABS Assessment Tool:

Please refer to Chapter 3 of the **TABS Manual** for important information before administering the TABS Assessment Tool. Complete (or have rater complete) the information in Section I. Read and discuss directions for Section II with the rater, making sure that he or she understands how to respond to the items. Ask the rater to return the Assessment Tool for scoring and interpretation when he or she has completed Section II.

I. CHILD INFORMATION

Name of child: ____________________ Sex: Female ❑ Male ❑

Date of birth: ____________________ Age (in years and months): __________

Child's address: ____________________

Name of parent or primary caregiver in household: ____________________

Relationship to child: Mother ❑ Father ❑ Other ____________________

Telephone number: ____________________ Best time to contact: __________

List any previously identified problems or diagnoses for this child.

1. ____________________
2. ____________________
3. ____________________

II. TABS INDICATORS

The following 55 items list some of the most frequent problems in temperament and self-regulation that parents and professionals observe in young children. Read each numbered item and check *No* if the behavior is not a problem. Check *Yes* if the behavior is a problem. For those items marked *Yes*, check *Need Help* if there is special concern and assistance is needed to cope with the behavior. Return this form to the individual administering this Assessment Tool for scoring and interpretation.

Name of rater: ____________________ Date Assessment Tool completed: __________

Relationship to child: ____________________

1-800-638-3775 www.brookespublishing.com

DETACHED	No	Yes	Need Help
1. Consistently upset by changes in schedule	☐	☐	☐
2. Emotions don't match what is going on	☐	☐	☐
3. Seems to look through or past people	☐	☐	☐
4. Resists looking you in the eye	☐	☐	☐
5. Acts like others are not there	☐	☐	☐
6. Hardly ever starts on own to play with others	☐	☐	☐
7. Moods and wants are too hard to figure out	☐	☐	☐
8. Seems to be in "own world"	☐	☐	☐
9. Often stares into space	☐	☐	☐
10. "Tunes out," loses contact with what is going on	☐	☐	☐
11. Plays with toys in strange ways	☐	☐	☐
12. Plays with toys as if confused by how they work	☐	☐	☐
13. Makes strange throat noises	☐	☐	☐
14. Disturbed by too much light, noise, or touching	☐	☐	☐
15. Overexcited in crowded places	☐	☐	☐
16. Stares at lights	☐	☐	☐
17. Overly interested in toy/object	☐	☐	☐
18. Flaps hands over and over	☐	☐	☐
19. Shakes head over and over	☐	☐	☐
20. Wanders around without purpose	☐	☐	☐
Detached Raw Score →		☐	

HYPER-SENSITIVE/ACTIVE	No	Yes	Need Help
21. Upset by every little thing	☐	☐	☐
22. Often difficult to soothe when upset and crying	☐	☐	☐
23. Has wide swings in mood	☐	☐	☐
24. Gets angry too easily	☐	☐	☐
25. Too easily frustrated	☐	☐	☐
26. Has wild temper tantrums	☐	☐	☐
27. Frequently irritable, "touchy," or fussy	☐	☐	☐
28. Can't wait at all for food or toy	☐	☐	☐
29. Demands attention continually	☐	☐	☐
30. Controls adult's behavior, "is the boss"	☐	☐	☐

	No	Yes	Need Help
31. Jealous too often	☐	☐	☐
32. Mostly on the go, "in high gear"	☐	☐	☐
33. Doesn't sit still	☐	☐	☐
34. Too "grabby," impulsive	☐	☐	☐
35. Almost always refuses to do what is told	☐	☐	☐
36. Throws or breaks things on purpose	☐	☐	☐
37. Bites, hits, kicks others	☐	☐	☐
Hyper-sensitive/active Raw Score →		☐	

UNDERREACTIVE

	No	Yes	Need Help
38. Rarely smiles, giggles, or laughs at funny things	☐	☐	☐
39. Doesn't pay attention to sights and sounds	☐	☐	☐
40. Doesn't seem to watch moving objects	☐	☐	☐
41. Shows no surprise to new events	☐	☐	☐
42. Doesn't react to own name	☐	☐	☐
43. Doesn't care when others are hurt	☐	☐	☐
44. Doesn't play much at all	☐	☐	☐
45. Doesn't enjoy playing with mother or caregiver	☐	☐	☐
46. Isn't upset when toy is taken away	☐	☐	☐
47. Almost never babbles or tries to talk	☐	☐	☐
48. Doesn't react to sounds	☐	☐	☐
Underreactive Raw Score →		☐	

DYSREGULATED

	No	Yes	Need Help
49. Often cries too long	☐	☐	☐
50. Often frightened by dreams or the nighttime	☐	☐	☐
51. Screams in sleep and can't be comforted	☐	☐	☐
52. Can't comfort self when upset	☐	☐	☐
53. Wakes up often and doesn't fall back asleep	☐	☐	☐
54. Doesn't have a regular sleep schedule	☐	☐	☐
55. Too often needs help to fall asleep	☐	☐	☐
Dysregulated Raw Score →		☐	

III. RESULTS

Add the items marked *Yes* in each of the four subtests, and place the totals in the appropriate boxes marked Raw Score (e.g., *Detached Raw Score*) after each subtest. Transfer those totals to the spaces under the column titled Raw Scores below. Add the four raw scores to calculate the *Temperament & Regulatory Index (TRI)*, and place it in the space provided. Determine percentiles and standard scores (or T-scores) of each of these raw scores by using the Conversion Table in the appendix in the **TABS Manual**. (Refer to Chapter 3 of the manual for a discussion of score conversions.) Although not intended for routine assessment purposes, subtest scores might be useful for research or highly specialized clinical purposes. If using subtest scores, carefully review Chapter 4 for information about subtest reliability and the reliability of differences between subtests. If the child's *TRI* indicates that he or she may be at risk for atypical development, early intervention and/or further assessment may be necessary.

	Raw Scores	Percentiles	Standard Scores (or T-scores)
Detached	....	....	....
Hyper-sensitive/active	....	....	....
Underreactive	....	....	....
Dysregulated	....	....	....
Temperament & Regulatory Index (TRI) (total of four factor raw scores)	________	________	________

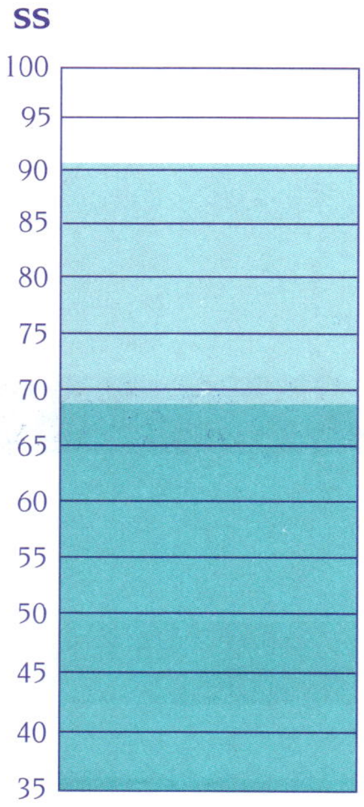

NOTES:

SS = Standard Score (*M* =100, *SD* =15)

☐ Typical ☐ At-Risk ☐ Atypical

ISBN-13: 978-1-55766-424-2 ISBN-10: 1-55766-424-2
Manufactured in the United States of America.

TABS Assessment Tool

Temperament and Atypical Behavior Scale

Early Childhood Indicators of Developmental Dysfunction

Stephen J. Bagnato, Ed.D., N.C.S.P. | John T. Neisworth, Ph.D.
John Salvia, D.Ed. | Frances M. Hunt, Ph.D.

Instructions for administering the TABS Assessment Tool:

Please refer to Chapter 3 of the **TABS Manual** for important information before administering the TABS Assessment Tool. Complete (or have rater complete) the information in Section I. Read and discuss directions for Section II with the rater, making sure that he or she understands how to respond to the items. Ask the rater to return the Assessment Tool for scoring and interpretation when he or she has completed Section II.

I. CHILD INFORMATION

Name of child: ______________________ Sex: Female ❑ Male ❑

Date of birth: ______________________ Age (in years and months): ______________

Child's address: ____

Name of parent or primary caregiver in household: ______________________

Relationship to child: Mother ❑ Father ❑ Other ______________________

Telephone number: ______________________ Best time to contact: ______________

List any previously identified problems or diagnoses for this child.

1. ____
2. ____
3. ____

II. TABS INDICATORS

The following 55 items list some of the most frequent problems in temperament and self-regulation that parents and professionals observe in young children. Read each numbered item and check *No* if the behavior is not a problem. Check *Yes* if the behavior is a problem. For those items marked *Yes*, check *Need Help* if there is special concern and assistance is needed to cope with the behavior. Return this form to the individual administering this Assessment Tool for scoring and interpretation.

Name of rater: ______________________ Date Assessment Tool completed: ______________

Relationship to child: ____

1-800-638-3775 www.brookespublishing.com

DETACHED	No	Yes	Need Help
1. Consistently upset by changes in schedule	☐	☐	☐
2. Emotions don't match what is going on	☐	☐	☐
3. Seems to look through or past people	☐	☐	☐
4. Resists looking you in the eye	☐	☐	☐
5. Acts like others are not there	☐	☐	☐
6. Hardly ever starts on own to play with others	☐	☐	☐
7. Moods and wants are too hard to figure out	☐	☐	☐
8. Seems to be in "own world"	☐	☐	☐
9. Often stares into space	☐	☐	☐
10. "Tunes out," loses contact with what is going on	☐	☐	☐
11. Plays with toys in strange ways	☐	☐	☐
12. Plays with toys as if confused by how they work	☐	☐	☐
13. Makes strange throat noises	☐	☐	☐
14. Disturbed by too much light, noise, or touching	☐	☐	☐
15. Overexcited in crowded places	☐	☐	☐
16. Stares at lights	☐	☐	☐
17. Overly interested in toy/object	☐	☐	☐
18. Flaps hands over and over	☐	☐	☐
19. Shakes head over and over	☐	☐	☐
20. Wanders around without purpose	☐	☐	☐
Detached Raw Score →		☐	

HYPER-SENSITIVE/ACTIVE	No	Yes	Need Help
21. Upset by every little thing	☐	☐	☐
22. Often difficult to soothe when upset and crying	☐	☐	☐
23. Has wide swings in mood	☐	☐	☐
24. Gets angry too easily	☐	☐	☐
25. Too easily frustrated	☐	☐	☐
26. Has wild temper tantrums	☐	☐	☐
27. Frequently irritable, "touchy," or fussy	☐	☐	☐
28. Can't wait at all for food or toy	☐	☐	☐
29. Demands attention continually	☐	☐	☐
30. Controls adult's behavior, "is the boss"	☐	☐	☐

	No	Yes	Need Help
31. Jealous too often	☐	☐	☐
32. Mostly on the go, "in high gear"	☐	☐	☐
33. Doesn't sit still	☐	☐	☐
34. Too "grabby," impulsive	☐	☐	☐
35. Almost always refuses to do what is told	☐	☐	☐
36. Throws or breaks things on purpose	☐	☐	☐
37. Bites, hits, kicks others	☐	☐	☐

Hyper-sensitive/active Raw Score → ☐

UNDERREACTIVE

	No	Yes	Need Help
38. Rarely smiles, giggles, or laughs at funny things	☐	☐	☐
39. Doesn't pay attention to sights and sounds	☐	☐	☐
40. Doesn't seem to watch moving objects	☐	☐	☐
41. Shows no surprise to new events	☐	☐	☐
42. Doesn't react to own name	☐	☐	☐
43. Doesn't care when others are hurt	☐	☐	☐
44. Doesn't play much at all	☐	☐	☐
45. Doesn't enjoy playing with mother or caregiver	☐	☐	☐
46. Isn't upset when toy is taken away	☐	☐	☐
47. Almost never babbles or tries to talk	☐	☐	☐
48. Doesn't react to sounds	☐	☐	☐

Underreactive Raw Score → ☐

DYSREGULATED

	No	Yes	Need Help
49. Often cries too long	☐	☐	☐
50. Often frightened by dreams or the nighttime	☐	☐	☐
51. Screams in sleep and can't be comforted	☐	☐	☐
52. Can't comfort self when upset	☐	☐	☐
53. Wakes up often and doesn't fall back asleep	☐	☐	☐
54. Doesn't have a regular sleep schedule	☐	☐	☐
55. Too often needs help to fall asleep	☐	☐	☐

Dysregulated Raw Score → ☐

III. RESULTS

Add the items marked *Yes* in each of the four subtests, and place the totals in the appropriate boxes marked Raw Score (e.g., *Detached Raw Score*) after each subtest. Transfer those totals to the spaces under the column titled Raw Scores below. Add the four raw scores to calculate the *Temperament & Regulatory Index (TRI)*, and place it in the space provided. Determine percentiles and standard scores (or T-scores) of each of these raw scores by using the Conversion Table in the appendix in the **TABS Manual**. (Refer to Chapter 3 of the manual for a discussion of score conversions.) Although not intended for routine assessment purposes, subtest scores might be useful for research or highly specialized clinical purposes. If using subtest scores, carefully review Chapter 4 for information about subtest reliability and the reliability of differences between subtests. If the child's *TRI* indicates that he or she may be at risk for atypical development, early intervention and/or further assessment may be necessary.

	Raw Scores	Percentiles	Standard Scores (or T-scores)
Detached			
Hyper-sensitive/active			
Underreactive			
Dysregulated			
Temperament & Regulatory Index (TRI) (total of four factor raw scores)			

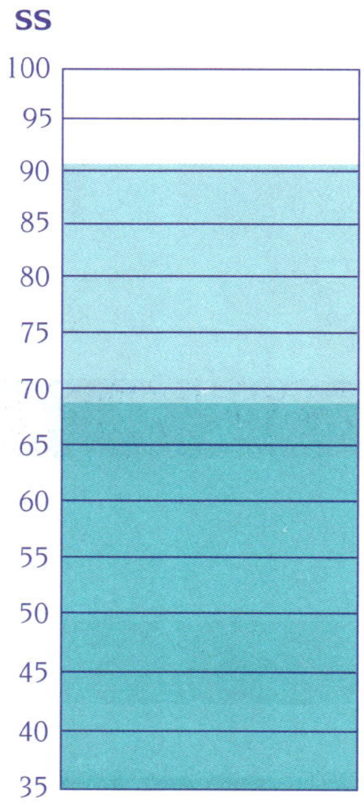

NOTES:

SS = Standard Score (M =100, SD =15)

☐ Typical ☐ At-Risk ☐ Atypical

 ISBN-13: 978-1-55766-424-2 ISBN-10: 1-55766-424-2
Manufactured in the United States of America.

TABS Assessment Tool

Temperament and Atypical Behavior Scale

Early Childhood Indicators of Developmental Dysfunction

Stephen J. Bagnato, Ed.D., N.C.S.P. | John T. Neisworth, Ph.D.

John Salvia, D.Ed. | Frances M. Hunt, Ph.D.

Instructions for administering the TABS Assessment Tool:

Please refer to Chapter 3 of the **TABS Manual** for important information before administering the TABS Assessment Tool. Complete (or have rater complete) the information in Section I. Read and discuss directions for Section II with the rater, making sure that he or she understands how to respond to the items. Ask the rater to return the Assessment Tool for scoring and interpretation when he or she has completed Section II.

I. CHILD INFORMATION

Name of child: ______________________ Sex: Female ❑ Male ❑

Date of birth: ______________________ Age (in years and months): ______________

Child's address: ______________________

Name of parent or primary caregiver in household: ______________________

Relationship to child: Mother ❑ Father ❑ Other ______________________

Telephone number: ______________________ Best time to contact: ______________

List any previously identified problems or diagnoses for this child.

1. ______________________
2. ______________________
3. ______________________

II. TABS INDICATORS

The following 55 items list some of the most frequent problems in temperament and self-regulation that parents and professionals observe in young children. Read each numbered item and check *No* if the behavior is not a problem. Check *Yes* if the behavior is a problem. For those items marked *Yes*, check *Need Help* if there is special concern and assistance is needed to cope with the behavior. Return this form to the individual administering this Assessment Tool for scoring and interpretation.

Name of rater: ______________________ Date Assessment Tool completed: ______________

Relationship to child: ______________________

1-800-638-3775 www.brookespublishing.com

DETACHED	No	Yes	Need Help
1. Consistently upset by changes in schedule	☐	☐	☐
2. Emotions don't match what is going on	☐	☐	☐
3. Seems to look through or past people	☐	☐	☐
4. Resists looking you in the eye	☐	☐	☐
5. Acts like others are not there	☐	☐	☐
6. Hardly ever starts on own to play with others	☐	☐	☐
7. Moods and wants are too hard to figure out	☐	☐	☐
8. Seems to be in "own world"	☐	☐	☐
9. Often stares into space	☐	☐	☐
10. "Tunes out," loses contact with what is going on	☐	☐	☐
11. Plays with toys in strange ways	☐	☐	☐
12. Plays with toys as if confused by how they work	☐	☐	☐
13. Makes strange throat noises	☐	☐	☐
14. Disturbed by too much light, noise, or touching	☐	☐	☐
15. Overexcited in crowded places	☐	☐	☐
16. Stares at lights	☐	☐	☐
17. Overly interested in toy/object	☐	☐	☐
18. Flaps hands over and over	☐	☐	☐
19. Shakes head over and over	☐	☐	☐
20. Wanders around without purpose	☐	☐	☐
Detached Raw Score →		☐	

HYPER-SENSITIVE/ACTIVE	No	Yes	Need Help
21. Upset by every little thing	☐	☐	☐
22. Often difficult to soothe when upset and crying	☐	☐	☐
23. Has wide swings in mood	☐	☐	☐
24. Gets angry too easily	☐	☐	☐
25. Too easily frustrated	☐	☐	☐
26. Has wild temper tantrums	☐	☐	☐
27. Frequently irritable, "touchy," or fussy	☐	☐	☐
28. Can't wait at all for food or toy	☐	☐	☐
29. Demands attention continually	☐	☐	☐
30. Controls adult's behavior, "is the boss"	☐	☐	☐

	No	Yes	Need Help
31. Jealous too often	☐	☐	☐
32. Mostly on the go, "in high gear"	☐	☐	☐
33. Doesn't sit still	☐	☐	☐
34. Too "grabby," impulsive	☐	☐	☐
35. Almost always refuses to do what is told	☐	☐	☐
36. Throws or breaks things on purpose	☐	☐	☐
37. Bites, hits, kicks others	☐	☐	☐
Hyper-sensitive/active Raw Score →		☐	

UNDERREACTIVE

	No	Yes	Need Help
38. Rarely smiles, giggles, or laughs at funny things	☐	☐	☐
39. Doesn't pay attention to sights and sounds	☐	☐	☐
40. Doesn't seem to watch moving objects	☐	☐	☐
41. Shows no surprise to new events	☐	☐	☐
42. Doesn't react to own name	☐	☐	☐
43. Doesn't care when others are hurt	☐	☐	☐
44. Doesn't play much at all	☐	☐	☐
45. Doesn't enjoy playing with mother or caregiver	☐	☐	☐
46. Isn't upset when toy is taken away	☐	☐	☐
47. Almost never babbles or tries to talk	☐	☐	☐
48. Doesn't react to sounds	☐	☐	☐
Underreactive Raw Score →		☐	

DYSREGULATED

	No	Yes	Need Help
49. Often cries too long	☐	☐	☐
50. Often frightened by dreams or the nighttime	☐	☐	☐
51. Screams in sleep and can't be comforted	☐	☐	☐
52. Can't comfort self when upset	☐	☐	☐
53. Wakes up often and doesn't fall back asleep	☐	☐	☐
54. Doesn't have a regular sleep schedule	☐	☐	☐
55. Too often needs help to fall asleep	☐	☐	☐
Dysregulated Raw Score →		☐	

III. RESULTS

Add the items marked *Yes* in each of the four subtests, and place the totals in the appropriate boxes marked Raw Score (e.g., *Detached Raw Score*) after each subtest. Transfer those totals to the spaces under the column titled Raw Scores below. Add the four raw scores to calculate the *Temperament & Regulatory Index (TRI)*, and place it in the space provided. Determine percentiles and standard scores (or T-scores) of each of these raw scores by using the Conversion Table in the appendix in the **TABS Manual**. (Refer to Chapter 3 of the manual for a discussion of score conversions.) Although not intended for routine assessment purposes, subtest scores might be useful for research or highly specialized clinical purposes. If using subtest scores, carefully review Chapter 4 for information about subtest reliability and the reliability of differences between subtests. If the child's *TRI* indicates that he or she may be at risk for atypical development, early intervention and/or further assessment may be necessary.

	Raw Scores	Percentiles	Standard Scores (or T-scores)
Detached	....	....	....
Hyper-sensitive/active	....	....	....
Underreactive	....	....	....
Dysregulated	....	....	....
Temperament & Regulatory Index (TRI) (total of four factor raw scores)	________	________	________

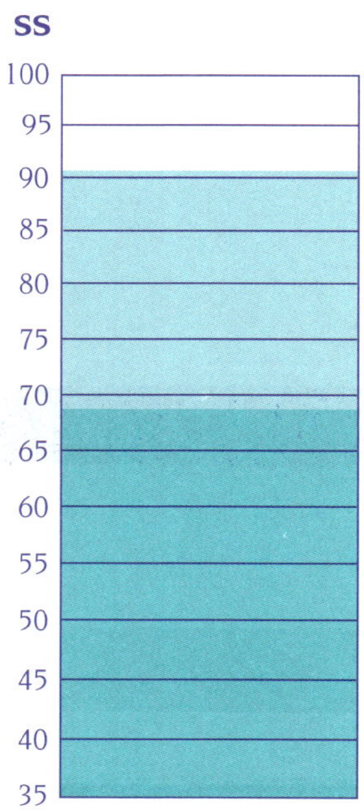

SS = Standard Score (*M* =100, *SD* =15)

☐ Typical ☐ At-Risk ☐ Atypical

NOTES:

 ISBN-13: 978-1-55766-424-2 ISBN-10: 1-55766-424-2
Manufactured in the United States of America.

TABS Assessment Tool

Temperament and Atypical Behavior Scale

Early Childhood Indicators of Developmental Dysfunction

Stephen J. Bagnato, Ed.D., N.C.S.P.
John T. Neisworth, Ph.D.
John Salvia, D.Ed.
Frances M. Hunt, Ph.D.

Instructions for administering the TABS Assessment Tool:

Please refer to Chapter 3 of the **TABS Manual** for important information before administering the TABS Assessment Tool. Complete (or have rater complete) the information in Section I. Read and discuss directions for Section II with the rater, making sure that he or she understands how to respond to the items. Ask the rater to return the Assessment Tool for scoring and interpretation when he or she has completed Section II.

I. CHILD INFORMATION

Name of child: ____________________ Sex: Female ☐ Male ☐

Date of birth: ____________________ Age (in years and months): __________

Child's address: ____________________

Name of parent or primary caregiver in household: ____________________

Relationship to child: Mother ☐ Father ☐ Other __________

Telephone number: ____________________ Best time to contact: __________

List any previously identified problems or diagnoses for this child.

1. ____________________
2. ____________________
3. ____________________

II. TABS INDICATORS

The following 55 items list some of the most frequent problems in temperament and self-regulation that parents and professionals observe in young children. Read each numbered item and check *No* if the behavior is not a problem. Check *Yes* if the behavior is a problem. For those items marked *Yes*, check *Need Help* if there is special concern and assistance is needed to cope with the behavior. Return this form to the individual administering this Assessment Tool for scoring and interpretation.

Name of rater: ____________________ Date Assessment Tool completed: __________

Relationship to child: ____________________

1-800-638-3775 www.brookespublishing.com

DETACHED	No	Yes	Need Help
1. Consistently upset by changes in schedule	☐	☐	☐
2. Emotions don't match what is going on	☐	☐	☐
3. Seems to look through or past people	☐	☐	☐
4. Resists looking you in the eye	☐	☐	☐
5. Acts like others are not there	☐	☐	☐
6. Hardly ever starts on own to play with others	☐	☐	☐
7. Moods and wants are too hard to figure out	☐	☐	☐
8. Seems to be in "own world"	☐	☐	☐
9. Often stares into space	☐	☐	☐
10. "Tunes out," loses contact with what is going on	☐	☐	☐
11. Plays with toys in strange ways	☐	☐	☐
12. Plays with toys as if confused by how they work	☐	☐	☐
13. Makes strange throat noises	☐	☐	☐
14. Disturbed by too much light, noise, or touching	☐	☐	☐
15. Overexcited in crowded places	☐	☐	☐
16. Stares at lights	☐	☐	☐
17. Overly interested in toy/object	☐	☐	☐
18. Flaps hands over and over	☐	☐	☐
19. Shakes head over and over	☐	☐	☐
20. Wanders around without purpose	☐	☐	☐
Detached Raw Score →		☐	

HYPER-SENSITIVE/ACTIVE	No	Yes	Need Help
21. Upset by every little thing	☐	☐	☐
22. Often difficult to soothe when upset and crying	☐	☐	☐
23. Has wide swings in mood	☐	☐	☐
24. Gets angry too easily	☐	☐	☐
25. Too easily frustrated	☐	☐	☐
26. Has wild temper tantrums	☐	☐	☐
27. Frequently irritable, "touchy," or fussy	☐	☐	☐
28. Can't wait at all for food or toy	☐	☐	☐
29. Demands attention continually	☐	☐	☐
30. Controls adult's behavior, "is the boss"	☐	☐	☐

	No	Yes	Need Help
31. Jealous too often	☐	☐	☐
32. Mostly on the go, "in high gear"	☐	☐	☐
33. Doesn't sit still	☐	☐	☐
34. Too "grabby," impulsive	☐	☐	☐
35. Almost always refuses to do what is told	☐	☐	☐
36. Throws or breaks things on purpose	☐	☐	☐
37. Bites, hits, kicks others	☐	☐	☐

Hyper-sensitive/active Raw Score → ☐

UNDERREACTIVE

	No	Yes	Need Help
38. Rarely smiles, giggles, or laughs at funny things	☐	☐	☐
39. Doesn't pay attention to sights and sounds	☐	☐	☐
40. Doesn't seem to watch moving objects	☐	☐	☐
41. Shows no surprise to new events	☐	☐	☐
42. Doesn't react to own name	☐	☐	☐
43. Doesn't care when others are hurt	☐	☐	☐
44. Doesn't play much at all	☐	☐	☐
45. Doesn't enjoy playing with mother or caregiver	☐	☐	☐
46. Isn't upset when toy is taken away	☐	☐	☐
47. Almost never babbles or tries to talk	☐	☐	☐
48. Doesn't react to sounds	☐	☐	☐

Underreactive Raw Score → ☐

DYSREGULATED

	No	Yes	Need Help
49. Often cries too long	☐	☐	☐
50. Often frightened by dreams or the nighttime	☐	☐	☐
51. Screams in sleep and can't be comforted	☐	☐	☐
52. Can't comfort self when upset	☐	☐	☐
53. Wakes up often and doesn't fall back asleep	☐	☐	☐
54. Doesn't have a regular sleep schedule	☐	☐	☐
55. Too often needs help to fall asleep	☐	☐	☐

Dysregulated Raw Score → ☐

III. RESULTS

Add the items marked *Yes* in each of the four subtests, and place the totals in the appropriate boxes marked Raw Score (e.g., *Detached Raw Score*) after each subtest. Transfer those totals to the spaces under the column titled Raw Scores below. Add the four raw scores to calculate the *Temperament & Regulatory Index (TRI)*, and place it in the space provided. Determine percentiles and standard scores (or T-scores) of each of these raw scores by using the Conversion Table in the appendix in the **TABS Manual**. (Refer to Chapter 3 of the manual for a discussion of score conversions.) Although not intended for routine assessment purposes, subtest scores might be useful for research or highly specialized clinical purposes. If using subtest scores, carefully review Chapter 4 for information about subtest reliability and the reliability of differences between subtests. If the child's *TRI* indicates that he or she may be at risk for atypical development, early intervention and/or further assessment may be necessary.

	Raw Scores	Percentiles	Standard Scores (or T-scores)
Detached	....	....	....
Hyper-sensitive/active	....	....	....
Underreactive	....	....	....
Dysregulated	....	....	....
Temperament & Regulatory Index (TRI) (total of four factor raw scores)	________	________	________

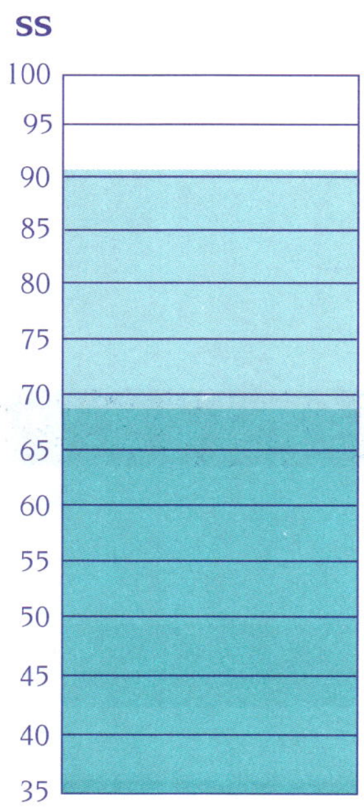

NOTES:

SS = Standard Score (*M* =100, *SD* =15)

☐ Typical ☐ At-Risk ☐ Atypical

 ISBN-13: 978-1-55766-424-2 ISBN-10: 1-55766-424-2
Manufactured in the United States of America.

TABS Assessment Tool

Temperament and Atypical Behavior Scale

Early Childhood Indicators of Developmental Dysfunction

Stephen J. Bagnato, Ed.D., N.C.S.P.
John T. Neisworth, Ph.D.
John Salvia, D.Ed.
Frances M. Hunt, Ph.D.

Instructions for administering the TABS Assessment Tool:

Please refer to Chapter 3 of the **TABS Manual** for important information before administering the TABS Assessment Tool. Complete (or have rater complete) the information in Section I. Read and discuss directions for Section II with the rater, making sure that he or she understands how to respond to the items. Ask the rater to return the Assessment Tool for scoring and interpretation when he or she has completed Section II.

I. CHILD INFORMATION

Name of child: ____________________ Sex: Female ❑ Male ❑

Date of birth: ____________________ Age (in years and months): ____________________

Child's address: ____________________

Name of parent or primary caregiver in household: ____________________

Relationship to child: Mother ❑ Father ❑ Other ____________________

Telephone number: ____________________ Best time to contact: ____________________

List any previously identified problems or diagnoses for this child.

1. ____________________
2. ____________________
3. ____________________

II. TABS INDICATORS

The following 55 items list some of the most frequent problems in temperament and self-regulation that parents and professionals observe in young children. Read each numbered item and check *No* if the behavior is not a problem. Check *Yes* if the behavior is a problem. For those items marked *Yes*, check *Need Help* if there is special concern and assistance is needed to cope with the behavior. Return this form to the individual administering this Assessment Tool for scoring and interpretation.

Name of rater: ____________________ Date Assessment Tool completed: ____________________

Relationship to child: ____________________

DETACHED

DETACHED	No	Yes	Need Help
1. Consistently upset by changes in schedule	☐	☐	☐
2. Emotions don't match what is going on	☐	☐	☐
3. Seems to look through or past people	☐	☐	☐
4. Resists looking you in the eye	☐	☐	☐
5. Acts like others are not there	☐	☐	☐
6. Hardly ever starts on own to play with others	☐	☐	☐
7. Moods and wants are too hard to figure out	☐	☐	☐
8. Seems to be in "own world"	☐	☐	☐
9. Often stares into space	☐	☐	☐
10. "Tunes out," loses contact with what is going on	☐	☐	☐
11. Plays with toys in strange ways	☐	☐	☐
12. Plays with toys as if confused by how they work	☐	☐	☐
13. Makes strange throat noises	☐	☐	☐
14. Disturbed by too much light, noise, or touching	☐	☐	☐
15. Overexcited in crowded places	☐	☐	☐
16. Stares at lights	☐	☐	☐
17. Overly interested in toy/object	☐	☐	☐
18. Flaps hands over and over	☐	☐	☐
19. Shakes head over and over	☐	☐	☐
20. Wanders around without purpose	☐	☐	☐

Detached Raw Score → ☐

HYPER-SENSITIVE/ACTIVE

HYPER-SENSITIVE/ACTIVE	No	Yes	Need Help
21. Upset by every little thing	☐	☐	☐
22. Often difficult to soothe when upset and crying	☐	☐	☐
23. Has wide swings in mood	☐	☐	☐
24. Gets angry too easily	☐	☐	☐
25. Too easily frustrated	☐	☐	☐
26. Has wild temper tantrums	☐	☐	☐
27. Frequently irritable, "touchy," or fussy	☐	☐	☐
28. Can't wait at all for food or toy	☐	☐	☐
29. Demands attention continually	☐	☐	☐
30. Controls adult's behavior, "is the boss"	☐	☐	☐

	No	Yes	Need Help
31. Jealous too often	☐	☐	☐
32. Mostly on the go, "in high gear"	☐	☐	☐
33. Doesn't sit still	☐	☐	☐
34. Too "grabby," impulsive	☐	☐	☐
35. Almost always refuses to do what is told	☐	☐	☐
36. Throws or breaks things on purpose	☐	☐	☐
37. Bites, hits, kicks others	☐	☐	☐

Hyper-sensitive/active Raw Score → ☐

UNDERREACTIVE

	No	Yes	Need Help
38. Rarely smiles, giggles, or laughs at funny things	☐	☐	☐
39. Doesn't pay attention to sights and sounds	☐	☐	☐
40. Doesn't seem to watch moving objects	☐	☐	☐
41. Shows no surprise to new events	☐	☐	☐
42. Doesn't react to own name	☐	☐	☐
43. Doesn't care when others are hurt	☐	☐	☐
44. Doesn't play much at all	☐	☐	☐
45. Doesn't enjoy playing with mother or caregiver	☐	☐	☐
46. Isn't upset when toy is taken away	☐	☐	☐
47. Almost never babbles or tries to talk	☐	☐	☐
48. Doesn't react to sounds	☐	☐	☐

Underreactive Raw Score → ☐

DYSREGULATED

	No	Yes	Need Help
49. Often cries too long	☐	☐	☐
50. Often frightened by dreams or the nighttime	☐	☐	☐
51. Screams in sleep and can't be comforted	☐	☐	☐
52. Can't comfort self when upset	☐	☐	☐
53. Wakes up often and doesn't fall back asleep	☐	☐	☐
54. Doesn't have a regular sleep schedule	☐	☐	☐
55. Too often needs help to fall asleep	☐	☐	☐

Dysregulated Raw Score → ☐

III. RESULTS

Add the items marked *Yes* in each of the four subtests, and place the totals in the appropriate boxes marked Raw Score (e.g., *Detached Raw Score*) after each subtest. Transfer those totals to the spaces under the column titled Raw Scores below. Add the four raw scores to calculate the *Temperament & Regulatory Index (TRI)*, and place it in the space provided. Determine percentiles and standard scores (or T-scores) of each of these raw scores by using the Conversion Table in the appendix in the **TABS Manual**. (Refer to Chapter 3 of the manual for a discussion of score conversions.) Although not intended for routine assessment purposes, subtest scores might be useful for research or highly specialized clinical purposes. If using subtest scores, carefully review Chapter 4 for information about subtest reliability and the reliability of differences between subtests. If the child's *TRI* indicates that he or she may be at risk for atypical development, early intervention and/or further assessment may be necessary.

	Raw Scores	Percentiles	Standard Scores (or T-scores)
Detached			
Hyper-sensitive/active			
Underreactive			
Dysregulated			
Temperament & Regulatory Index (TRI) (total of four factor raw scores)			

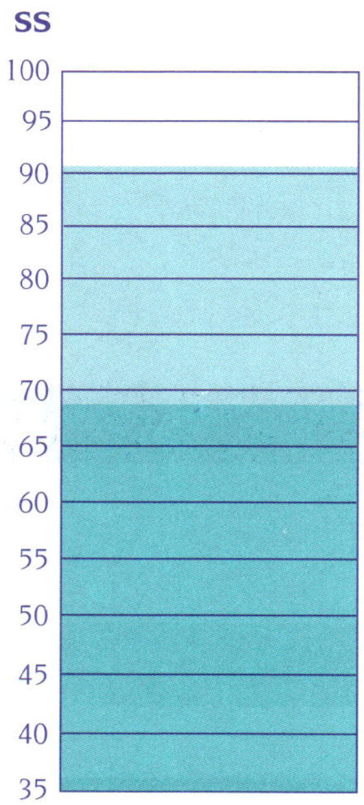

NOTES:

SS = Standard Score (*M* =100, *SD* =15)

☐ Typical ☐ At-Risk ☐ Atypical

 ISBN-13: 978-1-55766-424-2 ISBN-10: 1-55766-424-2
Manufactured in the United States of America.

TABS Assessment Tool

Temperament and Atypical Behavior Scale

Early Childhood Indicators of Developmental Dysfunction

Stephen J. Bagnato, Ed.D., N.C.S.P.
John T. Neisworth, Ph.D.
John Salvia, D.Ed.
Frances M. Hunt, Ph.D.

Instructions for administering the TABS Assessment Tool:

Please refer to Chapter 3 of the **TABS Manual** for important information before administering the TABS Assessment Tool. Complete (or have rater complete) the information in Section I. Read and discuss directions for Section II with the rater, making sure that he or she understands how to respond to the items. Ask the rater to return the Assessment Tool for scoring and interpretation when he or she has completed Section II.

I. CHILD INFORMATION

Name of child: ______________________ Sex: Female ❑ Male ❑

Date of birth: ______________________ Age (in years and months): ______________

Child's address: ______________________

Name of parent or primary caregiver in household: ______________________

Relationship to child: Mother ❑ Father ❑ Other ______________________

Telephone number: ______________________ Best time to contact: ______________

List any previously identified problems or diagnoses for this child.

1. ______________________
2. ______________________
3. ______________________

II. TABS INDICATORS

The following 55 items list some of the most frequent problems in temperament and self-regulation that parents and professionals observe in young children. Read each numbered item and check *No* if the behavior is not a problem. Check *Yes* if the behavior is a problem. For those items marked *Yes*, check *Need Help* if there is special concern and assistance is needed to cope with the behavior. Return this form to the individual administering this Assessment Tool for scoring and interpretation.

Name of rater: ______________________ Date Assessment Tool completed: ______________

Relationship to child: ______________________

DETACHED	No	Yes	Need Help
1. Consistently upset by changes in schedule	☐	☐	☐
2. Emotions don't match what is going on	☐	☐	☐
3. Seems to look through or past people	☐	☐	☐
4. Resists looking you in the eye	☐	☐	☐
5. Acts like others are not there	☐	☐	☐
6. Hardly ever starts on own to play with others	☐	☐	☐
7. Moods and wants are too hard to figure out	☐	☐	☐
8. Seems to be in "own world"	☐	☐	☐
9. Often stares into space	☐	☐	☐
10. "Tunes out," loses contact with what is going on	☐	☐	☐
11. Plays with toys in strange ways	☐	☐	☐
12. Plays with toys as if confused by how they work	☐	☐	☐
13. Makes strange throat noises	☐	☐	☐
14. Disturbed by too much light, noise, or touching	☐	☐	☐
15. Overexcited in crowded places	☐	☐	☐
16. Stares at lights	☐	☐	☐
17. Overly interested in toy/object	☐	☐	☐
18. Flaps hands over and over	☐	☐	☐
19. Shakes head over and over	☐	☐	☐
20. Wanders around without purpose	☐	☐	☐
Detached Raw Score →		☐	

HYPER-SENSITIVE/ACTIVE	No	Yes	Need Help
21. Upset by every little thing	☐	☐	☐
22. Often difficult to soothe when upset and crying	☐	☐	☐
23. Has wide swings in mood	☐	☐	☐
24. Gets angry too easily	☐	☐	☐
25. Too easily frustrated	☐	☐	☐
26. Has wild temper tantrums	☐	☐	☐
27. Frequently irritable, "touchy," or fussy	☐	☐	☐
28. Can't wait at all for food or toy	☐	☐	☐
29. Demands attention continually	☐	☐	☐
30. Controls adult's behavior, "is the boss"	☐	☐	☐

	No	Yes	Need Help
31. Jealous too often	☐	☐	☐
32. Mostly on the go, "in high gear"	☐	☐	☐
33. Doesn't sit still	☐	☐	☐
34. Too "grabby," impulsive	☐	☐	☐
35. Almost always refuses to do what is told	☐	☐	☐
36. Throws or breaks things on purpose	☐	☐	☐
37. Bites, hits, kicks others	☐	☐	☐

Hyper-sensitive/active Raw Score → ☐

UNDERREACTIVE

	No	Yes	Need Help
38. Rarely smiles, giggles, or laughs at funny things	☐	☐	☐
39. Doesn't pay attention to sights and sounds	☐	☐	☐
40. Doesn't seem to watch moving objects	☐	☐	☐
41. Shows no surprise to new events	☐	☐	☐
42. Doesn't react to own name	☐	☐	☐
43. Doesn't care when others are hurt	☐	☐	☐
44. Doesn't play much at all	☐	☐	☐
45. Doesn't enjoy playing with mother or caregiver	☐	☐	☐
46. Isn't upset when toy is taken away	☐	☐	☐
47. Almost never babbles or tries to talk	☐	☐	☐
48. Doesn't react to sounds	☐	☐	☐

Underreactive Raw Score → ☐

DYSREGULATED

	No	Yes	Need Help
49. Often cries too long	☐	☐	☐
50. Often frightened by dreams or the nighttime	☐	☐	☐
51. Screams in sleep and can't be comforted	☐	☐	☐
52. Can't comfort self when upset	☐	☐	☐
53. Wakes up often and doesn't fall back asleep	☐	☐	☐
54. Doesn't have a regular sleep schedule	☐	☐	☐
55. Too often needs help to fall asleep	☐	☐	☐

Dysregulated Raw Score → ☐

III. RESULTS

Add the items marked *Yes* in each of the four subtests, and place the totals in the appropriate boxes marked Raw Score (e.g., *Detached Raw Score*) after each subtest. Transfer those totals to the spaces under the column titled Raw Scores below. Add the four raw scores to calculate the *Temperament & Regulatory Index (TRI)*, and place it in the space provided. Determine percentiles and standard scores (or T-scores) of each of these raw scores by using the Conversion Table in the appendix in the **TABS Manual**. (Refer to Chapter 3 of the manual for a discussion of score conversions.) Although not intended for routine assessment purposes, subtest scores might be useful for research or highly specialized clinical purposes. If using subtest scores, carefully review Chapter 4 for information about subtest reliability and the reliability of differences between subtests. If the child's *TRI* indicates that he or she may be at risk for atypical development, early intervention and/or further assessment may be necessary.

	Raw Scores	Percentiles	Standard Scores (or T-scores)
Detached			
Hyper-sensitive/active			
Underreactive			
Dysregulated			
Temperament & Regulatory Index (TRI) (total of four factor raw scores)			

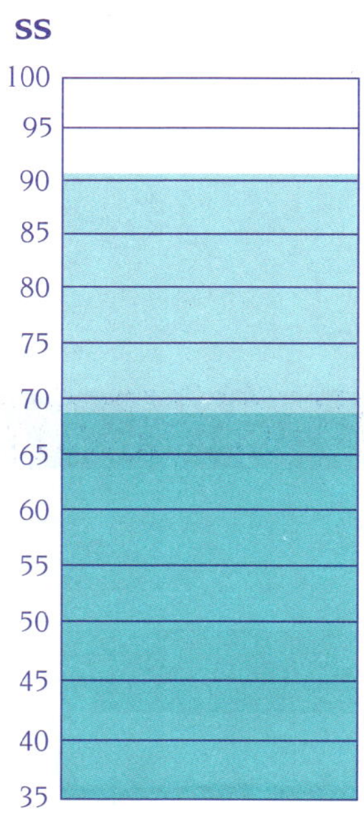

NOTES:

SS = Standard Score (*M* =100, *SD* =15)

☐ Typical ☐ At-Risk ☐ Atypical

 ISBN-13: 978-1-55766-424-2 ISBN-10: 1-55766-424-2
Manufactured in the United States of America.

TABS Assessment Tool

Temperament and Atypical Behavior Scale

Early Childhood Indicators of Developmental Dysfunction

Stephen J. Bagnato, Ed.D., N.C.S.P. | John T. Neisworth, Ph.D.
John Salvia, D.Ed. | Frances M. Hunt, Ph.D.

Instructions for administering the TABS Assessment Tool:
Please refer to Chapter 3 of the **TABS Manual** for important information before administering the TABS Assessment Tool. Complete (or have rater complete) the information in Section I. Read and discuss directions for Section II with the rater, making sure that he or she understands how to respond to the items. Ask the rater to return the Assessment Tool for scoring and interpretation when he or she has completed Section II.

I. CHILD INFORMATION

Name of child: ______________________ Sex: Female ❑ Male ❑

Date of birth: ______________________ Age (in years and months): ______________

Child's address: ______________________

Name of parent or primary caregiver in household: ______________________

Relationship to child: Mother ❑ Father ❑ Other ______________________

Telephone number: ______________________ Best time to contact: ______________

List any previously identified problems or diagnoses for this child.

1. ______________________
2. ______________________
3. ______________________

II. TABS INDICATORS

The following 55 items list some of the most frequent problems in temperament and self-regulation that parents and professionals observe in young children. Read each numbered item and check *No* if the behavior is not a problem. Check *Yes* if the behavior is a problem. For those items marked *Yes*, check *Need Help* if there is special concern and assistance is needed to cope with the behavior. Return this form to the individual administering this Assessment Tool for scoring and interpretation.

Name of rater: ______________________ Date Assessment Tool completed: ______________

Relationship to child: ______________________

1-800-638-3775 www.brookespublishing.com

DETACHED

	No	Yes	Need Help
1. Consistently upset by changes in schedule	☐	☐	☐
2. Emotions don't match what is going on	☐	☐	☐
3. Seems to look through or past people	☐	☐	☐
4. Resists looking you in the eye	☐	☐	☐
5. Acts like others are not there	☐	☐	☐
6. Hardly ever starts on own to play with others	☐	☐	☐
7. Moods and wants are too hard to figure out	☐	☐	☐
8. Seems to be in "own world"	☐	☐	☐
9. Often stares into space	☐	☐	☐
10. "Tunes out," loses contact with what is going on	☐	☐	☐
11. Plays with toys in strange ways	☐	☐	☐
12. Plays with toys as if confused by how they work	☐	☐	☐
13. Makes strange throat noises	☐	☐	☐
14. Disturbed by too much light, noise, or touching	☐	☐	☐
15. Overexcited in crowded places	☐	☐	☐
16. Stares at lights	☐	☐	☐
17. Overly interested in toy/object	☐	☐	☐
18. Flaps hands over and over	☐	☐	☐
19. Shakes head over and over	☐	☐	☐
20. Wanders around without purpose	☐	☐	☐

Detached Raw Score → ☐

HYPER-SENSITIVE/ACTIVE

	No	Yes	Need Help
21. Upset by every little thing	☐	☐	☐
22. Often difficult to soothe when upset and crying	☐	☐	☐
23. Has wide swings in mood	☐	☐	☐
24. Gets angry too easily	☐	☐	☐
25. Too easily frustrated	☐	☐	☐
26. Has wild temper tantrums	☐	☐	☐
27. Frequently irritable, "touchy," or fussy	☐	☐	☐
28. Can't wait at all for food or toy	☐	☐	☐
29. Demands attention continually	☐	☐	☐
30. Controls adult's behavior, "is the boss"	☐	☐	☐

	No	Yes	Need Help
31. Jealous too often	☐	☐	☐
32. Mostly on the go, "in high gear"	☐	☐	☐
33. Doesn't sit still	☐	☐	☐
34. Too "grabby," impulsive	☐	☐	☐
35. Almost always refuses to do what is told	☐	☐	☐
36. Throws or breaks things on purpose	☐	☐	☐
37. Bites, hits, kicks others	☐	☐	☐

Hyper-sensitive/active Raw Score → ☐

UNDERREACTIVE

	No	Yes	Need Help
38. Rarely smiles, giggles, or laughs at funny things	☐	☐	☐
39. Doesn't pay attention to sights and sounds	☐	☐	☐
40. Doesn't seem to watch moving objects	☐	☐	☐
41. Shows no surprise to new events	☐	☐	☐
42. Doesn't react to own name	☐	☐	☐
43. Doesn't care when others are hurt	☐	☐	☐
44. Doesn't play much at all	☐	☐	☐
45. Doesn't enjoy playing with mother or caregiver	☐	☐	☐
46. Isn't upset when toy is taken away	☐	☐	☐
47. Almost never babbles or tries to talk	☐	☐	☐
48. Doesn't react to sounds	☐	☐	☐

Underreactive Raw Score → ☐

DYSREGULATED

	No	Yes	Need Help
49. Often cries too long	☐	☐	☐
50. Often frightened by dreams or the nighttime	☐	☐	☐
51. Screams in sleep and can't be comforted	☐	☐	☐
52. Can't comfort self when upset	☐	☐	☐
53. Wakes up often and doesn't fall back asleep	☐	☐	☐
54. Doesn't have a regular sleep schedule	☐	☐	☐
55. Too often needs help to fall asleep	☐	☐	☐

Dysregulated Raw Score → ☐

III. RESULTS

Add the items marked *Yes* in each of the four subtests, and place the totals in the appropriate boxes marked Raw Score (e.g., *Detached Raw Score*) after each subtest. Transfer those totals to the spaces under the column titled Raw Scores below. Add the four raw scores to calculate the *Temperament & Regulatory Index (TRI)*, and place it in the space provided. Determine percentiles and standard scores (or T-scores) of each of these raw scores by using the Conversion Table in the appendix in the **TABS Manual**. (Refer to Chapter 3 of the manual for a discussion of score conversions.) Although not intended for routine assessment purposes, subtest scores might be useful for research or highly specialized clinical purposes. If using subtest scores, carefully review Chapter 4 for information about subtest reliability and the reliability of differences between subtests. If the child's *TRI* indicates that he or she may be at risk for atypical development, early intervention and/or further assessment may be necessary.

	Raw Scores	Percentiles	Standard Scores (or T-scores)
Detached			
Hyper-sensitive/active			
Underreactive			
Dysregulated			
Temperament & Regulatory Index (TRI) (total of four factor raw scores)			

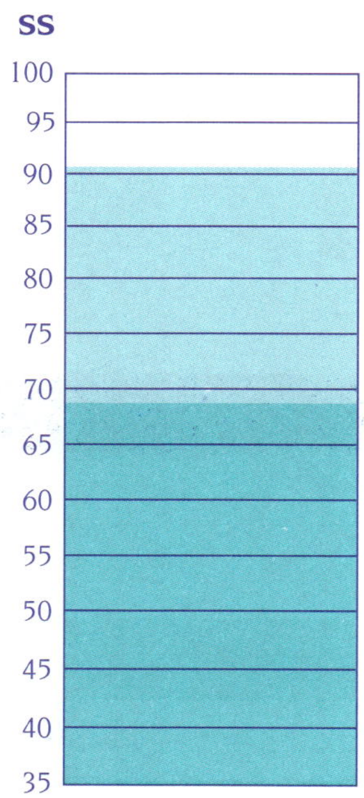

NOTES:

SS = Standard Score (*M* =100, *SD* =15)

☐ Typical ☐ At-Risk ☐ Atypical

 ISBN-13: 978-1-55766-424-2 ISBN-10: 1-55766-424-2
Manufactured in the United States of America.

TABS Assessment Tool

Temperament and Atypical Behavior Scale

Early Childhood Indicators of Developmental Dysfunction

Stephen J. Bagnato, Ed.D., N.C.S.P. | John T. Neisworth, Ph.D.
John Salvia, D.Ed. | Frances M. Hunt, Ph.D.

Instructions for administering the TABS Assessment Tool:

Please refer to Chapter 3 of the **TABS Manual** for important information before administering the TABS Assessment Tool. Complete (or have rater complete) the information in Section I. Read and discuss directions for Section II with the rater, making sure that he or she understands how to respond to the items. Ask the rater to return the Assessment Tool for scoring and interpretation when he or she has completed Section II.

I. CHILD INFORMATION

Name of child: ______________________ Sex: Female ❑ Male ❑

Date of birth: ______________________ Age (in years and months): ____________

Child's address: ______________________

Name of parent or primary caregiver in household: ______________________

Relationship to child: Mother ❑ Father ❑ Other ______________________

Telephone number: ______________________ Best time to contact: ____________

List any previously identified problems or diagnoses for this child.

1. ______________________
2. ______________________
3. ______________________

II. TABS INDICATORS

The following 55 items list some of the most frequent problems in temperament and self-regulation that parents and professionals observe in young children. Read each numbered item and check *No* if the behavior is not a problem. Check *Yes* if the behavior is a problem. For those items marked *Yes*, check *Need Help* if there is special concern and assistance is needed to cope with the behavior. Return this form to the individual administering this Assessment Tool for scoring and interpretation.

Name of rater: ______________________ Date Assessment Tool completed: ____________

Relationship to child: ______________________

1-800-638-3775 www.brookespublishing.com

DETACHED	No	Yes	Need Help
1. Consistently upset by changes in schedule	☐	☐	☐
2. Emotions don't match what is going on	☐	☐	☐
3. Seems to look through or past people	☐	☐	☐
4. Resists looking you in the eye	☐	☐	☐
5. Acts like others are not there	☐	☐	☐
6. Hardly ever starts on own to play with others	☐	☐	☐
7. Moods and wants are too hard to figure out	☐	☐	☐
8. Seems to be in "own world"	☐	☐	☐
9. Often stares into space	☐	☐	☐
10. "Tunes out," loses contact with what is going on	☐	☐	☐
11. Plays with toys in strange ways	☐	☐	☐
12. Plays with toys as if confused by how they work	☐	☐	☐
13. Makes strange throat noises	☐	☐	☐
14. Disturbed by too much light, noise, or touching	☐	☐	☐
15. Overexcited in crowded places	☐	☐	☐
16. Stares at lights	☐	☐	☐
17. Overly interested in toy/object	☐	☐	☐
18. Flaps hands over and over	☐	☐	☐
19. Shakes head over and over	☐	☐	☐
20. Wanders around without purpose	☐	☐	☐

Detached Raw Score → ☐

HYPER-SENSITIVE/ACTIVE	No	Yes	Need Help
21. Upset by every little thing	☐	☐	☐
22. Often difficult to soothe when upset and crying	☐	☐	☐
23. Has wide swings in mood	☐	☐	☐
24. Gets angry too easily	☐	☐	☐
25. Too easily frustrated	☐	☐	☐
26. Has wild temper tantrums	☐	☐	☐
27. Frequently irritable, "touchy," or fussy	☐	☐	☐
28. Can't wait at all for food or toy	☐	☐	☐
29. Demands attention continually	☐	☐	☐
30. Controls adult's behavior, "is the boss"	☐	☐	☐

	No	Yes	Need Help
31. Jealous too often	☐	☐	☐
32. Mostly on the go, "in high gear"	☐	☐	☐
33. Doesn't sit still	☐	☐	☐
34. Too "grabby," impulsive	☐	☐	☐
35. Almost always refuses to do what is told	☐	☐	☐
36. Throws or breaks things on purpose	☐	☐	☐
37. Bites, hits, kicks others	☐	☐	☐
Hyper-sensitive/active Raw Score →		☐	

UNDERREACTIVE

	No	Yes	Need Help
38. Rarely smiles, giggles, or laughs at funny things	☐	☐	☐
39. Doesn't pay attention to sights and sounds	☐	☐	☐
40. Doesn't seem to watch moving objects	☐	☐	☐
41. Shows no surprise to new events	☐	☐	☐
42. Doesn't react to own name	☐	☐	☐
43. Doesn't care when others are hurt	☐	☐	☐
44. Doesn't play much at all	☐	☐	☐
45. Doesn't enjoy playing with mother or caregiver	☐	☐	☐
46. Isn't upset when toy is taken away	☐	☐	☐
47. Almost never babbles or tries to talk	☐	☐	☐
48. Doesn't react to sounds	☐	☐	☐
Underreactive Raw Score →		☐	

DYSREGULATED

	No	Yes	Need Help
49. Often cries too long	☐	☐	☐
50. Often frightened by dreams or the nighttime	☐	☐	☐
51. Screams in sleep and can't be comforted	☐	☐	☐
52. Can't comfort self when upset	☐	☐	☐
53. Wakes up often and doesn't fall back asleep	☐	☐	☐
54. Doesn't have a regular sleep schedule	☐	☐	☐
55. Too often needs help to fall asleep	☐	☐	☐
Dysregulated Raw Score →		☐	

III. RESULTS

Add the items marked *Yes* in each of the four subtests, and place the totals in the appropriate boxes marked Raw Score (e.g., *Detached Raw Score*) after each subtest. Transfer those totals to the spaces under the column titled Raw Scores below. Add the four raw scores to calculate the *Temperament & Regulatory Index (TRI)*, and place it in the space provided. Determine percentiles and standard scores (or T-scores) of each of these raw scores by using the Conversion Table in the appendix in the **TABS Manual**. (Refer to Chapter 3 of the manual for a discussion of score conversions.) Although not intended for routine assessment purposes, subtest scores might be useful for research or highly specialized clinical purposes. If using subtest scores, carefully review Chapter 4 for information about subtest reliability and the reliability of differences between subtests. If the child's *TRI* indicates that he or she may be at risk for atypical development, early intervention and/or further assessment may be necessary.

	Raw Scores	Percentiles	Standard Scores (or T-scores)
Detached	....	....	....
Hyper-sensitive/active	....	....	....
Underreactive	....	....	....
Dysregulated	....	....	....
Temperament & Regulatory Index (TRI) (total of four factor raw scores)	________	________	________

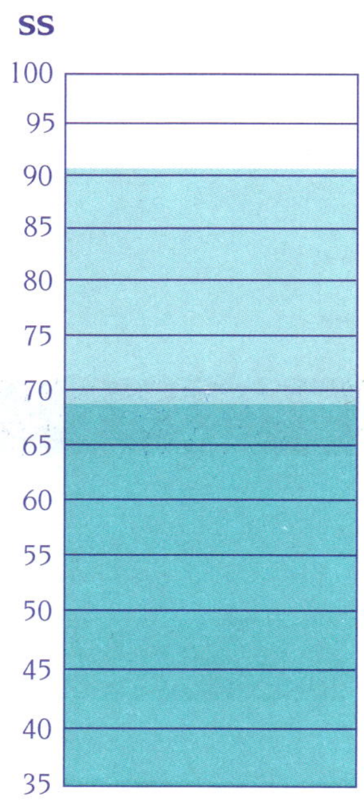

NOTES:

SS = Standard Score (*M* =100, *SD* =15)

☐ Typical ☐ At-Risk ☐ Atypical

 ISBN-13: 978-1-55766-424-2 ISBN-10: 1-55766-424-2
Manufactured in the United States of America.

TABS Assessment Tool

Temperament and Atypical Behavior Scale

Early Childhood Indicators of Developmental Dysfunction

Stephen J. Bagnato, Ed.D., N.C.S.P. | John T. Neisworth, Ph.D.
John Salvia, D.Ed. | Frances M. Hunt, Ph.D.

Instructions for administering the TABS Assessment Tool:

Please refer to Chapter 3 of the **TABS Manual** for important information before administering the TABS Assessment Tool. Complete (or have rater complete) the information in Section I. Read and discuss directions for Section II with the rater, making sure that he or she understands how to respond to the items. Ask the rater to return the Assessment Tool for scoring and interpretation when he or she has completed Section II.

I. CHILD INFORMATION

Name of child: ______________________ Sex: Female ❑ Male ❑

Date of birth: ______________________ Age (in years and months): ______________

Child's address: ______________________

Name of parent or primary caregiver in household: ______________________

Relationship to child: Mother ❑ Father ❑ Other ______________________

Telephone number: ______________________ Best time to contact: ______________

List any previously identified problems or diagnoses for this child.

1. ______________________
2. ______________________
3. ______________________

II. TABS INDICATORS

The following 55 items list some of the most frequent problems in temperament and self-regulation that parents and professionals observe in young children. Read each numbered item and check *No* if the behavior is not a problem. Check *Yes* if the behavior is a problem. For those items marked *Yes*, check *Need Help* if there is special concern and assistance is needed to cope with the behavior. Return this form to the individual administering this Assessment Tool for scoring and interpretation.

Name of rater: ______________________ Date Assessment Tool completed: ______________

Relationship to child: ______________________

1-800-638-3775 www.brookespublishing.com

DETACHED	No	Yes	Need Help
1. Consistently upset by changes in schedule	☐	☐	☐
2. Emotions don't match what is going on	☐	☐	☐
3. Seems to look through or past people	☐	☐	☐
4. Resists looking you in the eye	☐	☐	☐
5. Acts like others are not there	☐	☐	☐
6. Hardly ever starts on own to play with others	☐	☐	☐
7. Moods and wants are too hard to figure out	☐	☐	☐
8. Seems to be in "own world"	☐	☐	☐
9. Often stares into space	☐	☐	☐
10. "Tunes out," loses contact with what is going on	☐	☐	☐
11. Plays with toys in strange ways	☐	☐	☐
12. Plays with toys as if confused by how they work	☐	☐	☐
13. Makes strange throat noises	☐	☐	☐
14. Disturbed by too much light, noise, or touching	☐	☐	☐
15. Overexcited in crowded places	☐	☐	☐
16. Stares at lights	☐	☐	☐
17. Overly interested in toy/object	☐	☐	☐
18. Flaps hands over and over	☐	☐	☐
19. Shakes head over and over	☐	☐	☐
20. Wanders around without purpose	☐	☐	☐
Detached Raw Score →		☐	

HYPER-SENSITIVE/ACTIVE	No	Yes	Need Help
21. Upset by every little thing	☐	☐	☐
22. Often difficult to soothe when upset and crying	☐	☐	☐
23. Has wide swings in mood	☐	☐	☐
24. Gets angry too easily	☐	☐	☐
25. Too easily frustrated	☐	☐	☐
26. Has wild temper tantrums	☐	☐	☐
27. Frequently irritable, "touchy," or fussy	☐	☐	☐
28. Can't wait at all for food or toy	☐	☐	☐
29. Demands attention continually	☐	☐	☐
30. Controls adult's behavior, "is the boss"	☐	☐	☐

	No	Yes	Need Help
31. Jealous too often	☐	☐	☐
32. Mostly on the go, "in high gear"	☐	☐	☐
33. Doesn't sit still	☐	☐	☐
34. Too "grabby," impulsive	☐	☐	☐
35. Almost always refuses to do what is told	☐	☐	☐
36. Throws or breaks things on purpose	☐	☐	☐
37. Bites, hits, kicks others	☐	☐	☐

Hyper-sensitive/active Raw Score → ☐

UNDERREACTIVE

	No	Yes	Need Help
38. Rarely smiles, giggles, or laughs at funny things	☐	☐	☐
39. Doesn't pay attention to sights and sounds	☐	☐	☐
40. Doesn't seem to watch moving objects	☐	☐	☐
41. Shows no surprise to new events	☐	☐	☐
42. Doesn't react to own name	☐	☐	☐
43. Doesn't care when others are hurt	☐	☐	☐
44. Doesn't play much at all	☐	☐	☐
45. Doesn't enjoy playing with mother or caregiver	☐	☐	☐
46. Isn't upset when toy is taken away	☐	☐	☐
47. Almost never babbles or tries to talk	☐	☐	☐
48. Doesn't react to sounds	☐	☐	☐

Underreactive Raw Score → ☐

DYSREGULATED

	No	Yes	Need Help
49. Often cries too long	☐	☐	☐
50. Often frightened by dreams or the nighttime	☐	☐	☐
51. Screams in sleep and can't be comforted	☐	☐	☐
52. Can't comfort self when upset	☐	☐	☐
53. Wakes up often and doesn't fall back asleep	☐	☐	☐
54. Doesn't have a regular sleep schedule	☐	☐	☐
55. Too often needs help to fall asleep	☐	☐	☐

Dysregulated Raw Score → ☐

III. RESULTS

Add the items marked *Yes* in each of the four subtests, and place the totals in the appropriate boxes marked Raw Score (e.g., *Detached Raw Score*) after each subtest. Transfer those totals to the spaces under the column titled Raw Scores below. Add the four raw scores to calculate the *Temperament & Regulatory Index (TRI)*, and place it in the space provided. Determine percentiles and standard scores (or T-scores) of each of these raw scores by using the Conversion Table in the appendix in the **TABS Manual**. (Refer to Chapter 3 of the manual for a discussion of score conversions.) Although not intended for routine assessment purposes, subtest scores might be useful for research or highly specialized clinical purposes. If using subtest scores, carefully review Chapter 4 for information about subtest reliability and the reliability of differences between subtests. If the child's *TRI* indicates that he or she may be at risk for atypical development, early intervention and/or further assessment may be necessary.

	Raw Scores	Percentiles	Standard Scores (or T-scores)
Detached	....	....	....
Hyper-sensitive/active	....	....	....
Underreactive	....	....	....
Dysregulated	....	....	....
Temperament & Regulatory Index (TRI) (total of four factor raw scores)	________	________	________

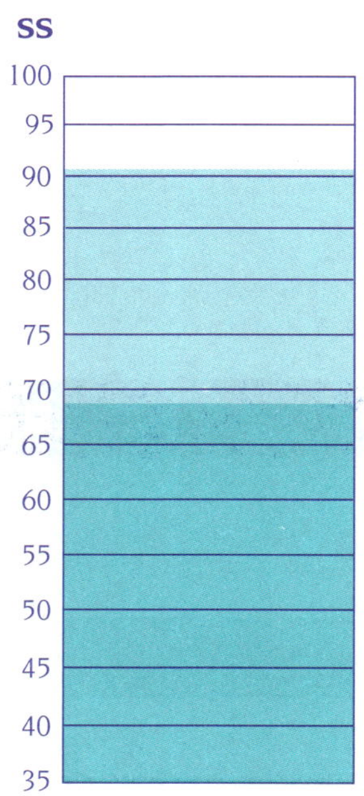

NOTES:

SS = Standard Score (M =100, SD =15)

☐ Typical ☐ At-Risk ☐ Atypical

 ISBN-13: 978-1-55766-424-2 ISBN-10: 1-55766-424-2
Manufactured in the United States of America.

TABS Assessment Tool

Temperament and Atypical Behavior Scale

Early Childhood Indicators of Developmental Dysfunction

Stephen J. Bagnato, Ed.D., N.C.S.P.
John T. Neisworth, Ph.D.
John Salvia, D.Ed.
Frances M. Hunt, Ph.D.

Instructions for administering the TABS Assessment Tool:

Please refer to Chapter 3 of the **TABS Manual** for important information before administering the TABS Assessment Tool. Complete (or have rater complete) the information in Section I. Read and discuss directions for Section II with the rater, making sure that he or she understands how to respond to the items. Ask the rater to return the Assessment Tool for scoring and interpretation when he or she has completed Section II.

I. CHILD INFORMATION

Name of child: ______________________ Sex: Female ❑ Male ❑

Date of birth: ______________________ Age (in years and months): ____________

Child's address: ______________________

Name of parent or primary caregiver in household: ______________________

Relationship to child: Mother ❑ Father ❑ Other ______________________

Telephone number: ______________________ Best time to contact: ____________

List any previously identified problems or diagnoses for this child.

1. ______________________
2. ______________________
3. ______________________

II. TABS INDICATORS

The following 55 items list some of the most frequent problems in temperament and self-regulation that parents and professionals observe in young children. Read each numbered item and check *No* if the behavior is not a problem. Check *Yes* if the behavior is a problem. For those items marked *Yes*, check *Need Help* if there is special concern and assistance is needed to cope with the behavior. Return this form to the individual administering this Assessment Tool for scoring and interpretation.

Name of rater: ______________________ Date Assessment Tool completed: ____________

Relationship to child: ______________________

DETACHED	No	Yes	Need Help
1. Consistently upset by changes in schedule	☐	☐	☐
2. Emotions don't match what is going on	☐	☐	☐
3. Seems to look through or past people	☐	☐	☐
4. Resists looking you in the eye	☐	☐	☐
5. Acts like others are not there	☐	☐	☐
6. Hardly ever starts on own to play with others	☐	☐	☐
7. Moods and wants are too hard to figure out	☐	☐	☐
8. Seems to be in "own world"	☐	☐	☐
9. Often stares into space	☐	☐	☐
10. "Tunes out," loses contact with what is going on	☐	☐	☐
11. Plays with toys in strange ways	☐	☐	☐
12. Plays with toys as if confused by how they work	☐	☐	☐
13. Makes strange throat noises	☐	☐	☐
14. Disturbed by too much light, noise, or touching	☐	☐	☐
15. Overexcited in crowded places	☐	☐	☐
16. Stares at lights	☐	☐	☐
17. Overly interested in toy/object	☐	☐	☐
18. Flaps hands over and over	☐	☐	☐
19. Shakes head over and over	☐	☐	☐
20. Wanders around without purpose	☐	☐	☐
Detached Raw Score →		☐	

HYPER-SENSITIVE/ACTIVE	No	Yes	Need Help
21. Upset by every little thing	☐	☐	☐
22. Often difficult to soothe when upset and crying	☐	☐	☐
23. Has wide swings in mood	☐	☐	☐
24. Gets angry too easily	☐	☐	☐
25. Too easily frustrated	☐	☐	☐
26. Has wild temper tantrums	☐	☐	☐
27. Frequently irritable, "touchy," or fussy	☐	☐	☐
28. Can't wait at all for food or toy	☐	☐	☐
29. Demands attention continually	☐	☐	☐
30. Controls adult's behavior, "is the boss"	☐	☐	☐

	No	Yes	Need Help
31. Jealous too often	☐	☐	☐
32. Mostly on the go, "in high gear"	☐	☐	☐
33. Doesn't sit still	☐	☐	☐
34. Too "grabby," impulsive	☐	☐	☐
35. Almost always refuses to do what is told	☐	☐	☐
36. Throws or breaks things on purpose	☐	☐	☐
37. Bites, hits, kicks others	☐	☐	☐

Hyper-sensitive/active Raw Score → ☐

UNDERREACTIVE

	No	Yes	Need Help
38. Rarely smiles, giggles, or laughs at funny things	☐	☐	☐
39. Doesn't pay attention to sights and sounds	☐	☐	☐
40. Doesn't seem to watch moving objects	☐	☐	☐
41. Shows no surprise to new events	☐	☐	☐
42. Doesn't react to own name	☐	☐	☐
43. Doesn't care when others are hurt	☐	☐	☐
44. Doesn't play much at all	☐	☐	☐
45. Doesn't enjoy playing with mother or caregiver	☐	☐	☐
46. Isn't upset when toy is taken away	☐	☐	☐
47. Almost never babbles or tries to talk	☐	☐	☐
48. Doesn't react to sounds	☐	☐	☐

Underreactive Raw Score → ☐

DYSREGULATED

	No	Yes	Need Help
49. Often cries too long	☐	☐	☐
50. Often frightened by dreams or the nighttime	☐	☐	☐
51. Screams in sleep and can't be comforted	☐	☐	☐
52. Can't comfort self when upset	☐	☐	☐
53. Wakes up often and doesn't fall back asleep	☐	☐	☐
54. Doesn't have a regular sleep schedule	☐	☐	☐
55. Too often needs help to fall asleep	☐	☐	☐

Dysregulated Raw Score → ☐

III. RESULTS

Add the items marked *Yes* in each of the four subtests, and place the totals in the appropriate boxes marked Raw Score (e.g., *Detached Raw Score*) after each subtest. Transfer those totals to the spaces under the column titled Raw Scores below. Add the four raw scores to calculate the *Temperament & Regulatory Index (TRI)*, and place it in the space provided. Determine percentiles and standard scores (or T-scores) of each of these raw scores by using the Conversion Table in the appendix in the **TABS Manual**. (Refer to Chapter 3 of the manual for a discussion of score conversions.) Although not intended for routine assessment purposes, subtest scores might be useful for research or highly specialized clinical purposes. If using subtest scores, carefully review Chapter 4 for information about subtest reliability and the reliability of differences between subtests. If the child's *TRI* indicates that he or she may be at risk for atypical development, early intervention and/or further assessment may be necessary.

	Raw Scores	Percentiles	Standard Scores (or T-scores)
Detached	....	....	....
Hyper-sensitive/active	....	....	....
Underreactive	....	....	....
Dysregulated	....	....	....
Temperament & Regulatory Index (TRI) (total of four factor raw scores)	________	________	________

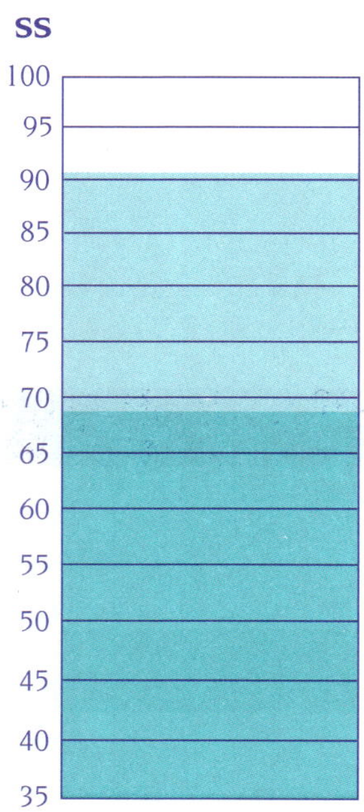

NOTES:

SS = Standard Score (*M* =100, *SD* =15)

☐ Typical ☐ At-Risk ☐ Atypical

 ISBN-13: 978-1-55766-424-2 ISBN-10: 1-55766-424-2
Manufactured in the United States of America.

TABS Assessment Tool

Temperament and Atypical Behavior Scale

Early Childhood Indicators of Developmental Dysfunction

Stephen J. Bagnato, Ed.D., N.C.S.P.
John T. Neisworth, Ph.D.
John Salvia, D.Ed.
Frances M. Hunt, Ph.D.

Instructions for administering the TABS Assessment Tool:

Please refer to Chapter 3 of the **TABS Manual** for important information before administering the TABS Assessment Tool. Complete (or have rater complete) the information in Section I. Read and discuss directions for Section II with the rater, making sure that he or she understands how to respond to the items. Ask the rater to return the Assessment Tool for scoring and interpretation when he or she has completed Section II.

I. CHILD INFORMATION

Name of child: ______________________ Sex: Female ☐ Male ☐

Date of birth: ______________________ Age (in years and months): ______________

Child's address: ______________________

Name of parent or primary caregiver in household: ______________________

Relationship to child: Mother ☐ Father ☐ Other ______________________

Telephone number: ______________________ Best time to contact: ______________

List any previously identified problems or diagnoses for this child.

1. ______________________
2. ______________________
3. ______________________

II. TABS INDICATORS

The following 55 items list some of the most frequent problems in temperament and self-regulation that parents and professionals observe in young children. Read each numbered item and check *No* if the behavior is not a problem. Check *Yes* if the behavior is a problem. For those items marked *Yes*, check *Need Help* if there is special concern and assistance is needed to cope with the behavior. Return this form to the individual administering this Assessment Tool for scoring and interpretation.

Name of rater: ______________________ Date Assessment Tool completed: ______________

Relationship to child: ______________________

DETACHED	No	Yes	Need Help
1. Consistently upset by changes in schedule	☐	☐	☐
2. Emotions don't match what is going on	☐	☐	☐
3. Seems to look through or past people	☐	☐	☐
4. Resists looking you in the eye	☐	☐	☐
5. Acts like others are not there	☐	☐	☐
6. Hardly ever starts on own to play with others	☐	☐	☐
7. Moods and wants are too hard to figure out	☐	☐	☐
8. Seems to be in "own world"	☐	☐	☐
9. Often stares into space	☐	☐	☐
10. "Tunes out," loses contact with what is going on	☐	☐	☐
11. Plays with toys in strange ways	☐	☐	☐
12. Plays with toys as if confused by how they work	☐	☐	☐
13. Makes strange throat noises	☐	☐	☐
14. Disturbed by too much light, noise, or touching	☐	☐	☐
15. Overexcited in crowded places	☐	☐	☐
16. Stares at lights	☐	☐	☐
17. Overly interested in toy/object	☐	☐	☐
18. Flaps hands over and over	☐	☐	☐
19. Shakes head over and over	☐	☐	☐
20. Wanders around without purpose	☐	☐	☐
Detached Raw Score →		☐	

HYPER-SENSITIVE/ACTIVE	No	Yes	Need Help
21. Upset by every little thing	☐	☐	☐
22. Often difficult to soothe when upset and crying	☐	☐	☐
23. Has wide swings in mood	☐	☐	☐
24. Gets angry too easily	☐	☐	☐
25. Too easily frustrated	☐	☐	☐
26. Has wild temper tantrums	☐	☐	☐
27. Frequently irritable, "touchy," or fussy	☐	☐	☐
28. Can't wait at all for food or toy	☐	☐	☐
29. Demands attention continually	☐	☐	☐
30. Controls adult's behavior, "is the boss"	☐	☐	☐

	No	Yes	Need Help
31. Jealous too often	☐	☐	☐
32. Mostly on the go, "in high gear"	☐	☐	☐
33. Doesn't sit still	☐	☐	☐
34. Too "grabby," impulsive	☐	☐	☐
35. Almost always refuses to do what is told	☐	☐	☐
36. Throws or breaks things on purpose	☐	☐	☐
37. Bites, hits, kicks others	☐	☐	☐
Hyper-sensitive/active Raw Score →		☐	

UNDERREACTIVE

	No	Yes	Need Help
38. Rarely smiles, giggles, or laughs at funny things	☐	☐	☐
39. Doesn't pay attention to sights and sounds	☐	☐	☐
40. Doesn't seem to watch moving objects	☐	☐	☐
41. Shows no surprise to new events	☐	☐	☐
42. Doesn't react to own name	☐	☐	☐
43. Doesn't care when others are hurt	☐	☐	☐
44. Doesn't play much at all	☐	☐	☐
45. Doesn't enjoy playing with mother or caregiver	☐	☐	☐
46. Isn't upset when toy is taken away	☐	☐	☐
47. Almost never babbles or tries to talk	☐	☐	☐
48. Doesn't react to sounds	☐	☐	☐
Underreactive Raw Score →		☐	

DYSREGULATED

	No	Yes	Need Help
49. Often cries too long	☐	☐	☐
50. Often frightened by dreams or the nighttime	☐	☐	☐
51. Screams in sleep and can't be comforted	☐	☐	☐
52. Can't comfort self when upset	☐	☐	☐
53. Wakes up often and doesn't fall back asleep	☐	☐	☐
54. Doesn't have a regular sleep schedule	☐	☐	☐
55. Too often needs help to fall asleep	☐	☐	☐
Dysregulated Raw Score →		☐	

III. RESULTS

Add the items marked *Yes* in each of the four subtests, and place the totals in the appropriate boxes marked Raw Score (e.g., *Detached Raw Score*) after each subtest. Transfer those totals to the spaces under the column titled Raw Scores below. Add the four raw scores to calculate the *Temperament & Regulatory Index (TRI)*, and place it in the space provided. Determine percentiles and standard scores (or T-scores) of each of these raw scores by using the Conversion Table in the appendix in the **TABS Manual**. (Refer to Chapter 3 of the manual for a discussion of score conversions.) Although not intended for routine assessment purposes, subtest scores might be useful for research or highly specialized clinical purposes. If using subtest scores, carefully review Chapter 4 for information about subtest reliability and the reliability of differences between subtests. If the child's *TRI* indicates that he or she may be at risk for atypical development, early intervention and/or further assessment may be necessary.

	Raw Scores	Percentiles	Standard Scores (or T-scores)
Detached	....	....	....
Hyper-sensitive/active	....	....	....
Underreactive	....	....	....
Dysregulated	....	....	....
Temperament & Regulatory Index (TRI) (total of four factor raw scores)	________	________	________

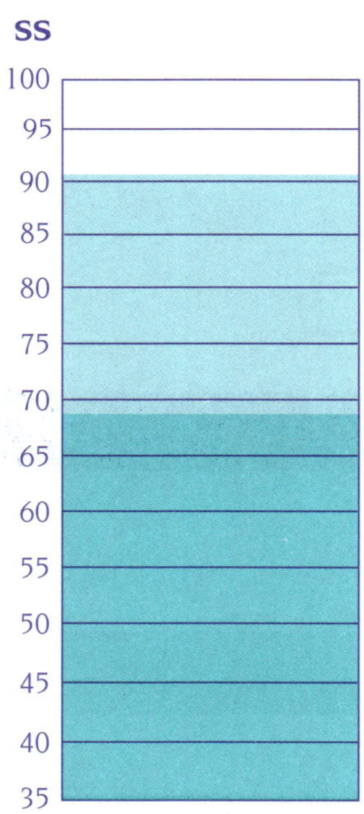

NOTES:

SS = Standard Score (M =100, SD =15)

☐ Typical ☐ At-Risk ☐ Atypical

 ISBN-13: 978-1-55766-424-2 ISBN-10: 1-55766-424-2
Manufactured in the United States of America.

TABS Assessment Tool

Temperament and Atypical Behavior Scale

Early Childhood Indicators of Developmental Dysfunction

Stephen J. Bagnato, Ed.D., N.C.S.P.
John T. Neisworth, Ph.D.
John Salvia, D.Ed.
Frances M. Hunt, Ph.D.

Instructions for administering the TABS Assessment Tool:

Please refer to Chapter 3 of the **TABS Manual** for important information before administering the TABS Assessment Tool. Complete (or have rater complete) the information in Section I. Read and discuss directions for Section II with the rater, making sure that he or she understands how to respond to the items. Ask the rater to return the Assessment Tool for scoring and interpretation when he or she has completed Section II.

I. CHILD INFORMATION

Name of child: ______________________ Sex: Female ❑ Male ❑

Date of birth: ______________________ Age (in years and months): ______________

Child's address: ______________________

Name of parent or primary caregiver in household: ______________________

Relationship to child: Mother ❑ Father ❑ Other ______________________

Telephone number: ______________________ Best time to contact: ______________

List any previously identified problems or diagnoses for this child.

1. ______________________
2. ______________________
3. ______________________

II. TABS INDICATORS

The following 55 items list some of the most frequent problems in temperament and self-regulation that parents and professionals observe in young children. Read each numbered item and check *No* if the behavior is not a problem. Check *Yes* if the behavior is a problem. For those items marked *Yes*, check *Need Help* if there is special concern and assistance is needed to cope with the behavior. Return this form to the individual administering this Assessment Tool for scoring and interpretation.

Name of rater: ______________________ Date Assessment Tool completed: ______________

Relationship to child: ______________________

1-800-638-3775 www.brookespublishing.com

DETACHED	No	Yes	Need Help
1. Consistently upset by changes in schedule	☐	☐	☐
2. Emotions don't match what is going on	☐	☐	☐
3. Seems to look through or past people	☐	☐	☐
4. Resists looking you in the eye	☐	☐	☐
5. Acts like others are not there	☐	☐	☐
6. Hardly ever starts on own to play with others	☐	☐	☐
7. Moods and wants are too hard to figure out	☐	☐	☐
8. Seems to be in "own world"	☐	☐	☐
9. Often stares into space	☐	☐	☐
10. "Tunes out," loses contact with what is going on	☐	☐	☐
11. Plays with toys in strange ways	☐	☐	☐
12. Plays with toys as if confused by how they work	☐	☐	☐
13. Makes strange throat noises	☐	☐	☐
14. Disturbed by too much light, noise, or touching	☐	☐	☐
15. Overexcited in crowded places	☐	☐	☐
16. Stares at lights	☐	☐	☐
17. Overly interested in toy/object	☐	☐	☐
18. Flaps hands over and over	☐	☐	☐
19. Shakes head over and over	☐	☐	☐
20. Wanders around without purpose	☐	☐	☐
Detached Raw Score →		☐	

HYPER-SENSITIVE/ACTIVE	No	Yes	Need Help
21. Upset by every little thing	☐	☐	☐
22. Often difficult to soothe when upset and crying	☐	☐	☐
23. Has wide swings in mood	☐	☐	☐
24. Gets angry too easily	☐	☐	☐
25. Too easily frustrated	☐	☐	☐
26. Has wild temper tantrums	☐	☐	☐
27. Frequently irritable, "touchy," or fussy	☐	☐	☐
28. Can't wait at all for food or toy	☐	☐	☐
29. Demands attention continually	☐	☐	☐
30. Controls adult's behavior, "is the boss"	☐	☐	☐

	No	Yes	Need Help
31. Jealous too often	☐	☐	☐
32. Mostly on the go, "in high gear"	☐	☐	☐
33. Doesn't sit still	☐	☐	☐
34. Too "grabby," impulsive	☐	☐	☐
35. Almost always refuses to do what is told	☐	☐	☐
36. Throws or breaks things on purpose	☐	☐	☐
37. Bites, hits, kicks others	☐	☐	☐

Hyper-sensitive/active Raw Score → ☐

UNDERREACTIVE

	No	Yes	Need Help
38. Rarely smiles, giggles, or laughs at funny things	☐	☐	☐
39. Doesn't pay attention to sights and sounds	☐	☐	☐
40. Doesn't seem to watch moving objects	☐	☐	☐
41. Shows no surprise to new events	☐	☐	☐
42. Doesn't react to own name	☐	☐	☐
43. Doesn't care when others are hurt	☐	☐	☐
44. Doesn't play much at all	☐	☐	☐
45. Doesn't enjoy playing with mother or caregiver	☐	☐	☐
46. Isn't upset when toy is taken away	☐	☐	☐
47. Almost never babbles or tries to talk	☐	☐	☐
48. Doesn't react to sounds	☐	☐	☐

Underreactive Raw Score → ☐

DYSREGULATED

	No	Yes	Need Help
49. Often cries too long	☐	☐	☐
50. Often frightened by dreams or the nighttime	☐	☐	☐
51. Screams in sleep and can't be comforted	☐	☐	☐
52. Can't comfort self when upset	☐	☐	☐
53. Wakes up often and doesn't fall back asleep	☐	☐	☐
54. Doesn't have a regular sleep schedule	☐	☐	☐
55. Too often needs help to fall asleep	☐	☐	☐

Dysregulated Raw Score → ☐

III. RESULTS

Add the items marked *Yes* in each of the four subtests, and place the totals in the appropriate boxes marked Raw Score (e.g., *Detached Raw Score*) after each subtest. Transfer those totals to the spaces under the column titled Raw Scores below. Add the four raw scores to calculate the *Temperament & Regulatory Index (TRI)*, and place it in the space provided. Determine percentiles and standard scores (or T-scores) of each of these raw scores by using the Conversion Table in the appendix in the **TABS Manual**. (Refer to Chapter 3 of the manual for a discussion of score conversions.) Although not intended for routine assessment purposes, subtest scores might be useful for research or highly specialized clinical purposes. If using subtest scores, carefully review Chapter 4 for information about subtest reliability and the reliability of differences between subtests. If the child's *TRI* indicates that he or she may be at risk for atypical development, early intervention and/or further assessment may be necessary.

	Raw Scores	Percentiles	Standard Scores (or T-scores)
Detached	....	....	....
Hyper-sensitive/active	....	....	....
Underreactive	....	....	....
Dysregulated	....	....	....
Temperament & Regulatory Index (TRI) (total of four factor raw scores)	____________	____________	____________

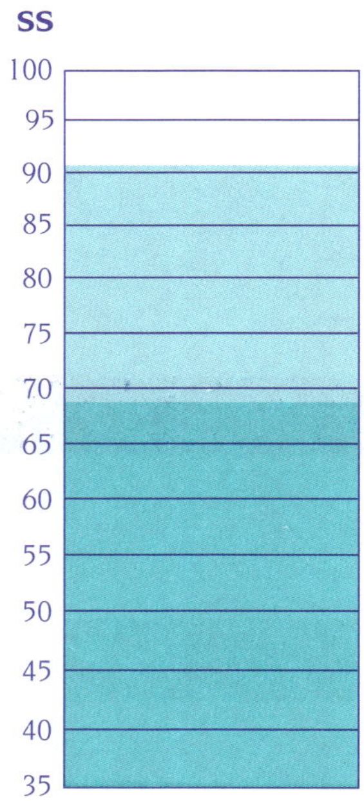

SS = Standard Score (M =100, SD =15)

☐ Typical ☐ At-Risk ☐ Atypical

NOTES:

 ISBN-13: 978-1-55766-424-2 ISBN-10: 1-55766-424-2
Manufactured in the United States of America.

TABS Assessment Tool

Temperament and Atypical Behavior Scale

Early Childhood Indicators of Developmental Dysfunction

Stephen J. Bagnato, Ed.D., N.C.S.P.
John T. Neisworth, Ph.D.
John Salvia, D.Ed.
Frances M. Hunt, Ph.D.

Instructions for administering the TABS Assessment Tool:

Please refer to Chapter 3 of the **TABS Manual** for important information before administering the TABS Assessment Tool. Complete (or have rater complete) the information in Section I. Read and discuss directions for Section II with the rater, making sure that he or she understands how to respond to the items. Ask the rater to return the Assessment Tool for scoring and interpretation when he or she has completed Section II.

I. CHILD INFORMATION

Name of child: ______________________ Sex: Female ☐ Male ☐

Date of birth: ______________________ Age (in years and months): ______________________

Child's address: ______________________

Name of parent or primary caregiver in household: ______________________

Relationship to child: Mother ☐ Father ☐ Other ______________________

Telephone number: ______________________ Best time to contact: ______________________

List any previously identified problems or diagnoses for this child.

1. ______________________
2. ______________________
3. ______________________

II. TABS INDICATORS

The following 55 items list some of the most frequent problems in temperament and self-regulation that parents and professionals observe in young children. Read each numbered item and check *No* if the behavior is not a problem. Check *Yes* if the behavior is a problem. For those items marked *Yes*, check *Need Help* if there is special concern and assistance is needed to cope with the behavior. Return this form to the individual administering this Assessment Tool for scoring and interpretation.

Name of rater: ______________________ Date Assessment Tool completed: ______________________

Relationship to child: ______________________

DETACHED	No	Yes	Need Help
1. Consistently upset by changes in schedule	☐	☐	☐
2. Emotions don't match what is going on	☐	☐	☐
3. Seems to look through or past people	☐	☐	☐
4. Resists looking you in the eye	☐	☐	☐
5. Acts like others are not there	☐	☐	☐
6. Hardly ever starts on own to play with others	☐	☐	☐
7. Moods and wants are too hard to figure out	☐	☐	☐
8. Seems to be in "own world"	☐	☐	☐
9. Often stares into space	☐	☐	☐
10. "Tunes out," loses contact with what is going on	☐	☐	☐
11. Plays with toys in strange ways	☐	☐	☐
12. Plays with toys as if confused by how they work	☐	☐	☐
13. Makes strange throat noises	☐	☐	☐
14. Disturbed by too much light, noise, or touching	☐	☐	☐
15. Overexcited in crowded places	☐	☐	☐
16. Stares at lights	☐	☐	☐
17. Overly interested in toy/object	☐	☐	☐
18. Flaps hands over and over	☐	☐	☐
19. Shakes head over and over	☐	☐	☐
20. Wanders around without purpose	☐	☐	☐
Detached Raw Score →		☐	

HYPER-SENSITIVE/ACTIVE	No	Yes	Need Help
21. Upset by every little thing	☐	☐	☐
22. Often difficult to soothe when upset and crying	☐	☐	☐
23. Has wide swings in mood	☐	☐	☐
24. Gets angry too easily	☐	☐	☐
25. Too easily frustrated	☐	☐	☐
26. Has wild temper tantrums	☐	☐	☐
27. Frequently irritable, "touchy," or fussy	☐	☐	☐
28. Can't wait at all for food or toy	☐	☐	☐
29. Demands attention continually	☐	☐	☐
30. Controls adult's behavior, "is the boss"	☐	☐	☐

	No	Yes	Need Help
31. Jealous too often	☐	☐	☐
32. Mostly on the go, "in high gear"	☐	☐	☐
33. Doesn't sit still	☐	☐	☐
34. Too "grabby," impulsive	☐	☐	☐
35. Almost always refuses to do what is told	☐	☐	☐
36. Throws or breaks things on purpose	☐	☐	☐
37. Bites, hits, kicks others	☐	☐	☐
Hyper-sensitive/active Raw Score →		☐	

UNDERREACTIVE

	No	Yes	Need Help
38. Rarely smiles, giggles, or laughs at funny things	☐	☐	☐
39. Doesn't pay attention to sights and sounds	☐	☐	☐
40. Doesn't seem to watch moving objects	☐	☐	☐
41. Shows no surprise to new events	☐	☐	☐
42. Doesn't react to own name	☐	☐	☐
43. Doesn't care when others are hurt	☐	☐	☐
44. Doesn't play much at all	☐	☐	☐
45. Doesn't enjoy playing with mother or caregiver	☐	☐	☐
46. Isn't upset when toy is taken away	☐	☐	☐
47. Almost never babbles or tries to talk	☐	☐	☐
48. Doesn't react to sounds	☐	☐	☐
Underreactive Raw Score →		☐	

DYSREGULATED

	No	Yes	Need Help
49. Often cries too long	☐	☐	☐
50. Often frightened by dreams or the nighttime	☐	☐	☐
51. Screams in sleep and can't be comforted	☐	☐	☐
52. Can't comfort self when upset	☐	☐	☐
53. Wakes up often and doesn't fall back asleep	☐	☐	☐
54. Doesn't have a regular sleep schedule	☐	☐	☐
55. Too often needs help to fall asleep	☐	☐	☐
Dysregulated Raw Score →		☐	

III. RESULTS

Add the items marked *Yes* in each of the four subtests, and place the totals in the appropriate boxes marked Raw Score (e.g., *Detached Raw Score*) after each subtest. Transfer those totals to the spaces under the column titled Raw Scores below. Add the four raw scores to calculate the *Temperament & Regulatory Index (TRI),* and place it in the space provided. Determine percentiles and standard scores (or T-scores) of each of these raw scores by using the Conversion Table in the appendix in the **TABS Manual**. (Refer to Chapter 3 of the manual for a discussion of score conversions.) Although not intended for routine assessment purposes, subtest scores might be useful for research or highly specialized clinical purposes. If using subtest scores, carefully review Chapter 4 for information about subtest reliability and the reliability of differences between subtests. If the child's *TRI* indicates that he or she may be at risk for atypical development, early intervention and/or further assessment may be necessary.

	Raw Scores	Percentiles	Standard Scores (or T-scores)
Detached	....	....	....
Hyper-sensitive/active	....	....	....
Underreactive	....	....	....
Dysregulated	....	....	....
Temperament & Regulatory Index (TRI) (total of four factor raw scores)	__________	__________	__________

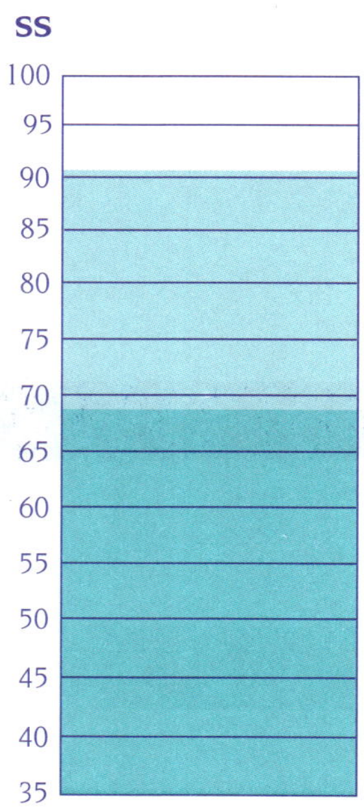

NOTES:

SS = Standard Score (*M* =100, *SD* =15)

☐ Typical ☐ At-Risk ☐ Atypical

 ISBN-13: 978-1-55766-424-2 ISBN-10: 1-55766-424-2
Manufactured in the United States of America.

TABS Assessment Tool

Temperament and Atypical Behavior Scale

Early Childhood Indicators of Developmental Dysfunction

Stephen J. Bagnato, Ed.D., N.C.S.P.
John T. Neisworth, Ph.D.
John Salvia, D.Ed.
Frances M. Hunt, Ph.D.

Instructions for administering the TABS Assessment Tool:

Please refer to Chapter 3 of the **TABS Manual** for important information before administering the TABS Assessment Tool. Complete (or have rater complete) the information in Section I. Read and discuss directions for Section II with the rater, making sure that he or she understands how to respond to the items. Ask the rater to return the Assessment Tool for scoring and interpretation when he or she has completed Section II.

I. CHILD INFORMATION

Name of child: ______________________ Sex: Female ❑ Male ❑

Date of birth: ______________________ Age (in years and months): ______________

Child's address: ______________________

Name of parent or primary caregiver in household: ______________________

Relationship to child: Mother ❑ Father ❑ Other ______________________

Telephone number: ______________________ Best time to contact: ______________

List any previously identified problems or diagnoses for this child.

1. ______________________
2. ______________________
3. ______________________

II. TABS INDICATORS

The following 55 items list some of the most frequent problems in temperament and self-regulation that parents and professionals observe in young children. Read each numbered item and check *No* if the behavior is not a problem. Check *Yes* if the behavior is a problem. For those items marked *Yes*, check *Need Help* if there is special concern and assistance is needed to cope with the behavior. Return this form to the individual administering this Assessment Tool for scoring and interpretation.

Name of rater: ______________________ Date Assessment Tool completed: ______________

Relationship to child: ______________________

1-800-638-3775 www.brookespublishing.com

DETACHED	No	Yes	Need Help
1. Consistently upset by changes in schedule	☐	☐	☐
2. Emotions don't match what is going on	☐	☐	☐
3. Seems to look through or past people	☐	☐	☐
4. Resists looking you in the eye	☐	☐	☐
5. Acts like others are not there	☐	☐	☐
6. Hardly ever starts on own to play with others	☐	☐	☐
7. Moods and wants are too hard to figure out	☐	☐	☐
8. Seems to be in "own world"	☐	☐	☐
9. Often stares into space	☐	☐	☐
10. "Tunes out," loses contact with what is going on	☐	☐	☐
11. Plays with toys in strange ways	☐	☐	☐
12. Plays with toys as if confused by how they work	☐	☐	☐
13. Makes strange throat noises	☐	☐	☐
14. Disturbed by too much light, noise, or touching	☐	☐	☐
15. Overexcited in crowded places	☐	☐	☐
16. Stares at lights	☐	☐	☐
17. Overly interested in toy/object	☐	☐	☐
18. Flaps hands over and over	☐	☐	☐
19. Shakes head over and over	☐	☐	☐
20. Wanders around without purpose	☐	☐	☐

Detached Raw Score → ☐

HYPER-SENSITIVE/ACTIVE	No	Yes	Need Help
21. Upset by every little thing	☐	☐	☐
22. Often difficult to soothe when upset and crying	☐	☐	☐
23. Has wide swings in mood	☐	☐	☐
24. Gets angry too easily	☐	☐	☐
25. Too easily frustrated	☐	☐	☐
26. Has wild temper tantrums	☐	☐	☐
27. Frequently irritable, "touchy," or fussy	☐	☐	☐
28. Can't wait at all for food or toy	☐	☐	☐
29. Demands attention continually	☐	☐	☐
30. Controls adult's behavior, "is the boss"	☐	☐	☐

	No	Yes	Need Help
31. Jealous too often	☐	☐	☐
32. Mostly on the go, "in high gear"	☐	☐	☐
33. Doesn't sit still	☐	☐	☐
34. Too "grabby," impulsive	☐	☐	☐
35. Almost always refuses to do what is told	☐	☐	☐
36. Throws or breaks things on purpose	☐	☐	☐
37. Bites, hits, kicks others	☐	☐	☐
Hyper-sensitive/active Raw Score →		☐	

UNDERREACTIVE

	No	Yes	Need Help
38. Rarely smiles, giggles, or laughs at funny things	☐	☐	☐
39. Doesn't pay attention to sights and sounds	☐	☐	☐
40. Doesn't seem to watch moving objects	☐	☐	☐
41. Shows no surprise to new events	☐	☐	☐
42. Doesn't react to own name	☐	☐	☐
43. Doesn't care when others are hurt	☐	☐	☐
44. Doesn't play much at all	☐	☐	☐
45. Doesn't enjoy playing with mother or caregiver	☐	☐	☐
46. Isn't upset when toy is taken away	☐	☐	☐
47. Almost never babbles or tries to talk	☐	☐	☐
48. Doesn't react to sounds	☐	☐	☐
Underreactive Raw Score →		☐	

DYSREGULATED

	No	Yes	Need Help
49. Often cries too long	☐	☐	☐
50. Often frightened by dreams or the nighttime	☐	☐	☐
51. Screams in sleep and can't be comforted	☐	☐	☐
52. Can't comfort self when upset	☐	☐	☐
53. Wakes up often and doesn't fall back asleep	☐	☐	☐
54. Doesn't have a regular sleep schedule	☐	☐	☐
55. Too often needs help to fall asleep	☐	☐	☐
Dysregulated Raw Score →		☐	

III. RESULTS

Add the items marked *Yes* in each of the four subtests, and place the totals in the appropriate boxes marked Raw Score (e.g., *Detached Raw Score*) after each subtest. Transfer those totals to the spaces under the column titled Raw Scores below. Add the four raw scores to calculate the *Temperament & Regulatory Index (TRI)*, and place it in the space provided. Determine percentiles and standard scores (or T-scores) of each of these raw scores by using the Conversion Table in the appendix in the **TABS Manual**. (Refer to Chapter 3 of the manual for a discussion of score conversions.) Although not intended for routine assessment purposes, subtest scores might be useful for research or highly specialized clinical purposes. If using subtest scores, carefully review Chapter 4 for information about subtest reliability and the reliability of differences between subtests. If the child's *TRI* indicates that he or she may be at risk for atypical development, early intervention and/or further assessment may be necessary.

	Raw Scores	Percentiles	Standard Scores (or T-scores)
Detached	....	....	....
Hyper-sensitive/active	....	....	....
Underreactive	....	....	....
Dysregulated	....	....	....
Temperament & Regulatory Index (TRI) (total of four factor raw scores)	________	________	________

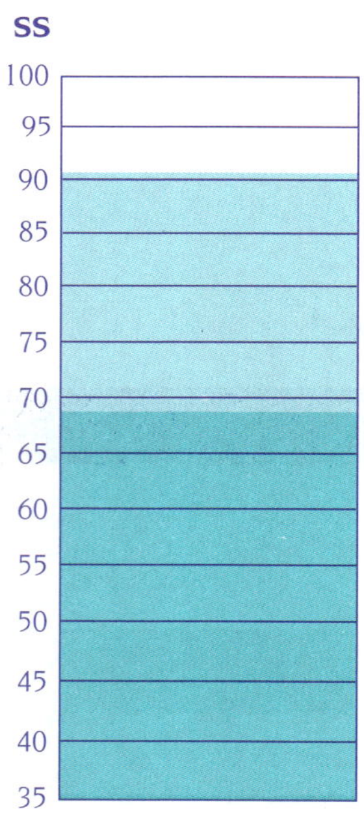

SS = Standard Score (*M* =100, *SD* =15)

☐ Typical ☐ At-Risk ☐ Atypical

NOTES:

ISBN-13: 978-1-55766-424-2 ISBN-10: 1-55766-424-2
Manufactured in the United States of America.

TABS Assessment Tool

Temperament and Atypical Behavior Scale

Early Childhood Indicators of Developmental Dysfunction

Stephen J. Bagnato, Ed.D., N.C.S.P.
John T. Neisworth, Ph.D.
John Salvia, D.Ed.
Frances M. Hunt, Ph.D.

Instructions for administering the TABS Assessment Tool:

Please refer to Chapter 3 of the **TABS Manual** for important information before administering the TABS Assessment Tool. Complete (or have rater complete) the information in Section I. Read and discuss directions for Section II with the rater, making sure that he or she understands how to respond to the items. Ask the rater to return the Assessment Tool for scoring and interpretation when he or she has completed Section II.

I. CHILD INFORMATION

Name of child: ______________________ Sex: Female ❑ Male ❑

Date of birth: ______________ Age (in years and months): ______________

Child's address: ______________________

Name of parent or primary caregiver in household: ______________________

Relationship to child: Mother ❑ Father ❑ Other ______________

Telephone number: ______________ Best time to contact: ______________

List any previously identified problems or diagnoses for this child.

1. ______________________
2. ______________________
3. ______________________

II. TABS INDICATORS

The following 55 items list some of the most frequent problems in temperament and self-regulation that parents and professionals observe in young children. Read each numbered item and check *No* if the behavior is not a problem. Check *Yes* if the behavior is a problem. For those items marked *Yes*, check *Need Help* if there is special concern and assistance is needed to cope with the behavior. Return this form to the individual administering this Assessment Tool for scoring and interpretation.

Name of rater: ______________ Date Assessment Tool completed: ______________

Relationship to child: ______________________

DETACHED

	No	Yes	Need Help
1. Consistently upset by changes in schedule	☐	☐	☐
2. Emotions don't match what is going on	☐	☐	☐
3. Seems to look through or past people	☐	☐	☐
4. Resists looking you in the eye	☐	☐	☐
5. Acts like others are not there	☐	☐	☐
6. Hardly ever starts on own to play with others	☐	☐	☐
7. Moods and wants are too hard to figure out	☐	☐	☐
8. Seems to be in "own world"	☐	☐	☐
9. Often stares into space	☐	☐	☐
10. "Tunes out," loses contact with what is going on	☐	☐	☐
11. Plays with toys in strange ways	☐	☐	☐
12. Plays with toys as if confused by how they work	☐	☐	☐
13. Makes strange throat noises	☐	☐	☐
14. Disturbed by too much light, noise, or touching	☐	☐	☐
15. Overexcited in crowded places	☐	☐	☐
16. Stares at lights	☐	☐	☐
17. Overly interested in toy/object	☐	☐	☐
18. Flaps hands over and over	☐	☐	☐
19. Shakes head over and over	☐	☐	☐
20. Wanders around without purpose	☐	☐	☐

Detached Raw Score → ☐

HYPER-SENSITIVE/ACTIVE

	No	Yes	Need Help
21. Upset by every little thing	☐	☐	☐
22. Often difficult to soothe when upset and crying	☐	☐	☐
23. Has wide swings in mood	☐	☐	☐
24. Gets angry too easily	☐	☐	☐
25. Too easily frustrated	☐	☐	☐
26. Has wild temper tantrums	☐	☐	☐
27. Frequently irritable, "touchy," or fussy	☐	☐	☐
28. Can't wait at all for food or toy	☐	☐	☐
29. Demands attention continually	☐	☐	☐
30. Controls adult's behavior, "is the boss"	☐	☐	☐

	No	Yes	Need Help
31. Jealous too often	☐	☐	☐
32. Mostly on the go, "in high gear"	☐	☐	☐
33. Doesn't sit still	☐	☐	☐
34. Too "grabby," impulsive	☐	☐	☐
35. Almost always refuses to do what is told	☐	☐	☐
36. Throws or breaks things on purpose	☐	☐	☐
37. Bites, hits, kicks others	☐	☐	☐
Hyper-sensitive/active Raw Score →		☐	

UNDERREACTIVE

	No	Yes	Need Help
38. Rarely smiles, giggles, or laughs at funny things	☐	☐	☐
39. Doesn't pay attention to sights and sounds	☐	☐	☐
40. Doesn't seem to watch moving objects	☐	☐	☐
41. Shows no surprise to new events	☐	☐	☐
42. Doesn't react to own name	☐	☐	☐
43. Doesn't care when others are hurt	☐	☐	☐
44. Doesn't play much at all	☐	☐	☐
45. Doesn't enjoy playing with mother or caregiver	☐	☐	☐
46. Isn't upset when toy is taken away	☐	☐	☐
47. Almost never babbles or tries to talk	☐	☐	☐
48. Doesn't react to sounds	☐	☐	☐
Underreactive Raw Score →		☐	

DYSREGULATED

	No	Yes	Need Help
49. Often cries too long	☐	☐	☐
50. Often frightened by dreams or the nighttime	☐	☐	☐
51. Screams in sleep and can't be comforted	☐	☐	☐
52. Can't comfort self when upset	☐	☐	☐
53. Wakes up often and doesn't fall back asleep	☐	☐	☐
54. Doesn't have a regular sleep schedule	☐	☐	☐
55. Too often needs help to fall asleep	☐	☐	☐
Dysregulated Raw Score →		☐	

III. RESULTS

Add the items marked *Yes* in each of the four subtests, and place the totals in the appropriate boxes marked Raw Score (e.g., *Detached Raw Score*) after each subtest. Transfer those totals to the spaces under the column titled Raw Scores below. Add the four raw scores to calculate the *Temperament & Regulatory Index (TRI)*, and place it in the space provided. Determine percentiles and standard scores (or T-scores) of each of these raw scores by using the Conversion Table in the appendix in the **TABS Manual**. (Refer to Chapter 3 of the manual for a discussion of score conversions.) Although not intended for routine assessment purposes, subtest scores might be useful for research or highly specialized clinical purposes. If using subtest scores, carefully review Chapter 4 for information about subtest reliability and the reliability of differences between subtests. If the child's *TRI* indicates that he or she may be at risk for atypical development, early intervention and/or further assessment may be necessary.

	Raw Scores	Percentiles	Standard Scores (or T-scores)
Detached	....	....	....
Hyper-sensitive/active	....	....	....
Underreactive	....	....	....
Dysregulated	....	....	....
Temperament & Regulatory Index (TRI) (total of four factor raw scores)	________	________	________

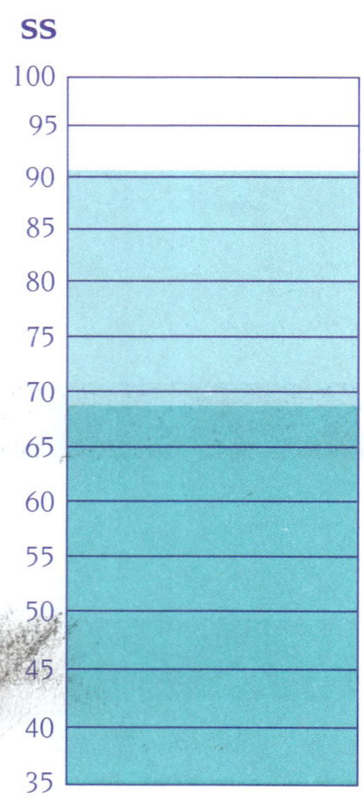

SS = Standard Score (*M* =100, *SD* =15)

☐ Typical ☐ At-Risk ☐ Atypical

NOTES:

ISBN-13: 978-1-55766-424-2
ISBN-10: 1-55766-424-2
90000>
9 781557 664242

 ISBN-13: 978-1-55766-424-2 ISBN-10: 1-55766-424-2
Manufactured in the United States of America.